THEOGONY

and

WORKS AND DAYS

THEOGONY

and

WORKS AND DAYS

Hesiod

Translated and with introductions by
CATHERINE M. SCHLEGEL *and*
HENRY WEINFIELD

THE UNIVERSITY OF MICHIGAN PRESS
Ann Arbor

Copyright © by the University of Michigan 2006
All rights reserved
Published in the United States of America by
The University of Michigan Press
Manufactured in the United States of America
⊗ Printed on acid-free paper
2010   2009   2008   2007   5   4   3   2

A CIP catalog record for this book is available from the British Library.

Hesiod.
    [Theogony. English.]
    Theogony ; and, Works and days / Hesiod ; translated and with
introductions by Catherine M. Schlegel and Henry Weinfield.
        p.   cm.
    Includes bibliographical references.
    ISBN-13: 978-0-472-09932-0 (cloth : alk. paper)
    ISBN-10: 0-472-09932-9 (cloth : alk. paper)
    ISBN-13: 978-0-472-06932-3 (pbk. : alk. paper)
    ISBN-10: 0-472-06932-2 (pbk. : alk. paper)
        1. Hesiod—Translations into English.   2. Religious poetry,
Greek—Translations into English.   3. Didactic poetry, Greek—
Translations into English.   4. Agriculture—Greece—Poetry.
    5. Gods, Greek—Poetry.   I. Schlegel, Catherine.   II. Weinfield, Henry.
III. Hesiod. Works and days. English.   IV. Title: Works and days.
V. Title.
    PA4010.E5T5   2006
    881'.01—dc22   2006001566

Cover photograph
The Gales Painter
Potter: Gales
Oil flask (lekythos) with sacrificial procession (detail)
Greek, Archaic Period, about 520–510 B.C.
Place of Manufacture: Greece, Attica, Athens
Ceramic, Red Figure
Height: 31 cm (12 3/16 in.)
Museum of Fine Arts, Boston
Francis Barlett Donation of 1912, 13.195

TABLE OF CONTENTS

THEOGONY

and

WORKS AND DAYS

INTRODUCTION TO HESIOD

UNLIKE HOMER, WHOSE IDENTITY AS A POET IS SO OBSCURE
that it is sometimes proposed that he is a committee, Hesiod's distinctive voice in the *Theogony* (*Th*) and the *Works and Days* (*WD*)
delivers to us the first "poetic self" and depicts the first poetic
career in western literature. He is afraid of sailing, hates his hometown (Askra), has a brother and a father, entered a poetry contest,
and has (or reflects) significant anxieties about women. Most of this
information comes from the *Works and Days,* because the didactic
genre exploits the first-person speaker's authority. However, even
in the *Theogony* the poet's relation to the Muses has a personal edge
that makes the invocation's generic appeal Hesiod's particular call.

The view that Homer (that is, the poet conventionally known
as the author of the *Iliad* and the *Odyssey*) was earlier than Hesiod
has recently given way to some skepticism, but in any case the
poems of both, in the form we have them written, date from
between 750 and 600 BCE. Hesiod and Homer were paired in
antiquity, as they are today, as the great epic poets of the Greek
archaic era. To us their similarities seem few. For one thing, we
have no sense of the organizing power of the dactylic hexameter,

the meter in which Hesiod's and Homer's poems are composed and whose sound defined epic, nor of the Ionian dialect that was the characteristic speech of archaic Greek epic. To modern students "epic" as a genre suggests something big, usually historic, sometimes overblown; epic can fit the grand scope of Homer, but not Hesiod's comparative brevity (one book of the *Iliad* can be as long as the whole *Works and Days,* and the *Theogony* only exceeds it by two hundred lines). The heroic epic gave Milton the genre for *Paradise Lost,* the subject matter of which matched or exceeded the scope and weight of Homer's material, and gave it a length to echo Vergil's epic the *Aeneid,* a poem that itself consciously recalls Homer. Films such as *Lawrence of Arabia* or *Star Wars* claim the genre of epic for being concerned with heroes, history, the cosmos and its exploration, and the human values established and revealed by the stories they develop. But in archaic Greek poetry, epic contains, in addition to its heroic songs, short poems about the gods (such as the *Homeric Hymns,* or the song in the *Odyssey* that Demodocus sings to the Phaeacians about Ares and Aphrodite), systematic narratives such as the *Theogony,* and didactic poems such as the *Works and Days.*

Hesiod probably made use of writing in composing his poems, but his poems belong to the preliterate poetic tradition in which, for uncountable centuries before, poems were composed orally by singers and relied on the sound of the singing for their meaning; we are here a long way from the solitary, silent reader of modern poetry. Singers called rhapsodes traveled throughout the Greek world (mainland Greece, the islands, the coasts of Asia minor, and what is now Turkey), singing at festivals and special banquets (such as that in Phaeacia in the *Odyssey* book 8) and constituting an important and integral part of civilized life. We know from Hesiod (*Works and Days* 654–59) that he entered a contest and won the prize at a festival, where singers would have recited (or sung, accompanied by a lyre) poems that included portions of the saga of the Trojan war as well as poems such as Hesiod's own. Obviously such entertainment teaches and gives pleasure to its audience; as the rhapsode tells the tales of the gods and the heroic past he teaches the values and history of the Greeks, to the Greeks; the pleasure of song is the rare commodity that we mortals may share with the gods.

We can share that pleasure because the source of poetry is divine. The Muses, daughters of Zeus who delight their father with song, give the poet the ability to sing to mortals—and, in the process, give us what little portion of lasting fame we have. The poet must invoke the Muses so that they will teach him to sing and help him as he sings. In his long invocation at the beginning of the *Theogony,* Hesiod reports that the Muses "breathed a god-inspired voice in me, / That I might celebrate the things that were and that shall be." Homer never speaks in the first person, except to invoke the Muse for her help at the beginning of a song or in the special circumstance of remembering long lists and catalogues; but Hesiod's first-person pronoun, his poetic self, participates in the invocation of the Muses in the *Theogony* and even names him: "The Muses once to Hesiod taught lovely song indeed, / While he was tending to his sheep on holy Helicon." The singers of orally composed poetry sang songs that had been conceived, perfected, and re-perfected by singers over generations, and they undoubtedly altered these received poems according to the occasion of the performances and their own talents. But the song is not the singer's own, and the idea of a god who gives the performer the song is certainly as plausible as the idea of a god who gives you lightning bolts or justice or infinite mercy. Add to the unknown source of your song the peculiar psychology of poetic inspiration—unpredictable, frustrating, and uncanny even in the most secular of circumstances—and the idea that a divinity is responsible for the myriad elements of this art seems inescapable. However, if authorship (and even the idea of authorship is a new thing in a context where previously performance, not invention, must have been the focus) can be located in a particular singer's skill, inspired by the Muse, and, though composed within the conventions of oral poetry, verifiably a product special to this singer, the relationship of the singer to his song will be different than it was formerly, as we see that it is in Hesiod.

The sense that Hesiod has an identity comes from statements he makes that are attributable to the poet's persona—the biographical notes about his family, for instance. But it also comes from his distinct point of view as it shapes his telling of clearly conventional material, though his point of view is obviously controlled by the program of each poem. We learn more about Hesiod from the *Works and Days* than from the *Theogony* because the *Works and Days* is a didactic poem: the authoritative and explicitly avowed first-person speaker is a convention of the didactic style where a speaker directs his thoughts and injunctions to a second-person addressee—in the *Works and Days* to Hesiod's brother Perses. More broadly, where the *Theogony* is an account of the creation of a stable cosmos, the generations of the gods, and the reconciliation of divine family violence under the rule of Zeus, the *Works and Days* locates human life in that ordered cosmos and tells how to live justly under the rule of Zeus.

The two poems' differences in their accounts of the creation of the first woman illustrate their different orientations. In the *Theogony* the creation of the first woman is incidental to the quarrel between Zeus and Prometheus. The poem, one notes, tells a creation story that does not include the creation of humans but only of women; that men have existed alongside the gods until the time of the gift of fire is, remarkably, only revealed with the comment that at Mekone the gods and men were making some formal division among themselves (*Theogony* 535) when Prometheus devises his scheme to trick Zeus. That trick describes the etiology of sacrifice: Prometheus misleads Zeus—and the text is resolutely ambiguous about how fully Zeus was deceived—so that he takes the portion of the ox that is only bones but covered with the luscious-looking fat. In this model, when we mortals share a meal with the gods it will only be in the ritual meal of sacrifice; our portion will be the bloody, meaty parts—we will eat our mortality, in the phrase of J.-P. Vernant—while the sweet-smelling smoke rises up to nourish the gods. In anger at Prometheus for the fat-and-bones trick, Zeus keeps fire from humans, but Prometheus, a version of the trickster archetype, sneaks fire to mortals anyway and thus prompts Zeus's retaliatory creation of the first woman. This first woman has no name; Zeus orders her manufacture ("The lovely evil he had made to countervail the good" [*Theogony* 585]), Hephaistos makes her from clay, and Athena dresses her. She and her miraculous adornment are called "marvels," or marvelous to see, wonders that impress both gods and men. She is also a devouring, consuming woe to men; yet without her there are no children. Heterosexual reproduction is the price humans pay, at the hand of Zeus, for the civilizing force of fire; woman is the baleful counterweight to Prometheus's technological gift. The narrative then reverts to the conflict between Prometheus and Zeus, and to Zeus's conquest and his inescapable rage—but it is Prometheus who can't escape him; the men whose lives are altered entirely for the worse by the introduction of a woman into the previously all male world are, again, incidental to the larger purposes of this narrative.

In the *Works and Days* the first woman has a name, and she is part of the explanation of why men's lives are hard, why we must work, and why we need to be just; she is part of the program to explain the lives of humans in the cosmos under the rule of Zeus. The quarrel that occupied some fifty lines of narrative in the *Theogony*—the retaliatory exchanges of force (Zeus) and tricks (Prometheus)—is summarized in eight lines in the *Works and Days*; the malice of Zeus is greater, and he laughs aloud at the *idea* of the recompense for fire that he devises, before she is even made (*Works and Days* 59). While the woman is a marvel in the *Theogony,* the *Works and Days* devotes much more intimate detail to her making, appearance, and nature, why she is a threat to men, and how she is installed through Prometheus's unknowing human brother, Epimetheus, the man of afterthought. Her name is Pandora, which means "All-Gifted," both because all the gods give her gifts and because she has all gifts:

> And the gods' herald gave her a voice, by the thunderer's design,
> And called this woman the All-Gifted one, Pandora, because the
>   divine
> Olympians all gave her a gift and as a gift did give
> Her as a woe to mortal men, who must earn their bread to live.
> (Works and Days 79–82)

Aphrodite gives her "painful longing"; that is, Hesiod has the goddess put the male response to women *inside* the woman. Moreover, Pandora opens a jar (not a box, as conventional parlance would have it), a *pithos,* the ubiquitous ancient container that holds life-sustaining substances such as olive oil and grain and is rounded in the middle, shaped like a pregnant woman's body. Like Pandora, the *pithos* is made of clay. Ills go flying out of the jar—all the suffering that men had never known before the coming of women. But hope stays inside, beneath the rim of the jar. Hope is the unborn child inside a woman's belly, but whose child will it be? Implicit is the male's fear about the outcome of his desire for this beautiful maiden. The woman is a woe, an endless uncertainty, and her body embodies male desire.

Hesiod is sometimes cited as the prime and earliest example, the *locus classicus,* of ancient Greek misogyny. But it is worth noting that the reasons for the fear at the base of this misogyny are abundantly clear, and that Hesiod's animus against women is easy to deconstruct. In the *Theogony* the woman stays inside the house consuming goods, depleting the man; while men work all day, like bees, women, like drones, "stay within the sheltered hives and gather / Into their stomachs all the work expended by another" (*Theogony* 598–99). In the *Works and Days* the inside of the woman herself holds the mystery of the child, the ambiguous hope inside the jar: that hope is ambiguous because if the woman has *not* stayed inside his house the child may not be his. The *Theogony* demonstrates Zeus's construction of a patriarchy to block the cyclic episodes of birth, violence, and usurpation that manifest themselves in the first two divine generations. The very first generation needs no father, no male, and the earth, Gaia, gives birth on her own. In the last generation of gods Athena needs no mother, and Zeus's violence takes away female power over her own reproduction. The human order is located within the divine one: the power that women potentially hold is articulated clearly in both poems, and the concomitant male fear is reasonable in the circumstances of property inheritance as it is set up in a patriarchy. Hesiod's is, if one were choosing, a misogyny preferable to later literary forms of the phenomenon, that of the Roman elegiac poet, for instance, whose suave control of the female is so seamless that he enjoys depicting her rebellions. Hesiod reveals the causes and nature of his fear, and how the fear engenders mistrust and hatred; we thus recognize the defensive posture underlying the aggressive maneuvers and recognize that this is standard, lamentable human behavior, even when divine.

Women aside, property rights are still difficult. The didactic pose Hesiod strikes in the *Works and Days* rests upon a conflict between himself and his brother Perses over their inheritance from their father, and the conceit of the poem is that he directs his speech to his brother. Hesiod can thus invest the didactic poet's position of authority with personal emotion and can then broaden his scope from personal feeling to a general view of justice that delineates the human condition, explaining why we need justice and what are the rules of just living, down to our days and hours and weeks. Most of all, we see the difficulty of making a living off the unforgiving Greek soil. Hesiod's invocation to the Muses in this poem is worth comparing with his extraordinarily long invocation at the start of the *Theogony,* where some of his anxiety about women seems extended to the Muses, who use their human singers with ungenerous will, not revealing for certain whether or not they tell the truth. "You shepherds of the wilderness, mere bellies, poor excuse / For men," he has his Muses say to him: "we can make falsities and fallacies seem true, / But when we want we're able to give truthful statements too" (*Theogony* 24–28). The Muses are the only source of crucial gifts to humans; one of these is straight justice and fair speech by way of Zeus (*Theogony* 80–93)— what is so important in the conflict with Perses in the *Works and Days*—and the other is forgetfulness of anguish, the solace that hearing a singer brings to humans who suffer (*Theogony* 97–103). But while in the *Theogony* the singer's problem is being unable to know, being outside, in the *Works and Days* Hesiod invokes the Muses with no taint of mistrust. His invocation (and here it is only ten lines) opens with a triple speech-act: he calls upon the Muses, asking them to speak of Zeus; he enjoins the god to hear him; and he claims to Perses that he will speak only the truth. He makes a claim for justice and a claim for truth.

In this human world that needs the unambiguous Muse and the help of Zeus, Hesiod's distinction between the two kinds of Strife opens the exposition of the brothers' quarrel. Hesiod's description of Perses's greedy behavior, and that of others like him, culminates in one of his most vexed lines, "Fools, they don't know how much more the half is than the whole" (*Works and Days* 40). This is a moment that registers Hesiod's bleak recognition of human limitation: we are not gods and thus cannot have the whole; the half is our inevitable portion—and yet with Justice we can live with this, live without bad Strife, and have the better path. It is clear that many of Hesiod's sources for the didactic *Works and Days* belong to a much older tradition of wisdom literature, yet this verse is so typical of the poet in the *Works and Days,* who takes pains to reveal himself, that we have a window here into how the individual poet in the archaic period interacts with conventional material. "How much more the half is than the whole" has an aphoristic ring that is nevertheless Hesiod's own.

The identification in this century of Near Eastern texts—Mesopotamian, Egyptian, Sumerian, Hittite, and Semitic—that are clear sources for Hesiod's poetry also shows the eastward turn of the archaic Greek world, toward trade routes that are easier than westward ones, and toward older, more sophisticated civilizations than that of the Greeks. The story in the *Theogony* of the succession of the gods is a version of a far older Hittite tale, found in the Babylonian *Enuma Elish.* The wisdom literature of the Egyptians and Phoenicians is plainly evident in the *Works and Days,* and readers less learned in arcane literature will recognize echoes of Proverbs, Leviticus, or Genesis.

Hesiod's influence over ancient poetry was immense. His importance even to Plato is obvious from how frequently this writer of prose, who was of course deeply skeptical about poetry, quotes him. One of the most famous examples is Plato's Myth of the Metals in Book 3 of *The Republic,* where Hesiod's genetic myth of the different ages of men, from gold to iron, is transformed to an ontological myth (Plato's "noble lie") about the different *kinds* of men. Six or seven hundred years after Hesiod, in a profoundly different world, the Roman poets Vergil and Lucretius both wrote didactic poems that look back to Hesiod.

The poems as we have them are clearly not quite the ones Hesiod left. The evidence is good that neither the *Theogony* nor the *Works and Days* ended as they do now. The last hundred lines or so of the *Theogony* are certainly not by the same Hesiod who wrote the first nine hundred, and the *Works and Days* as we have it was, in the ancient world, followed by a discussion of bird omens. The endings of poems from antiquity are especially vulnerable to additions and substitutions. But in this translation we have treated the poems as the entities that their texts present today, and such is the supple, insistent grace of these poems, so closely do they still adhere to the Muses' inspiration, that Hesiod's voice seems as clear and compelling as it ever was. Our hope is to convey some of Hesiod's wonder.

I owe particular thanks in this project to Rebecca Resinski, whose careful reading of Hesiod exceeds any critic's I know for its clarity, truth, and generosity; her wisdom has informed a great deal of my own thinking about this most human yet magical poet.

Most classicists dream of translating their favorite poems into English, but most of us have skills rather more on the philological than the poetical side. I feel profound gratitude to Henry Weinfield for this collaboration, which, begun rather cavalierly and certainly by chance, has given me the opportunity to participate in changing Hesiod's astounding poems into what strikes me as equally astounding English. Henry Weinfield's alchemical gifts as a poet and thinker are responsible for an outcome to this collaboration that fulfills every hope I have had for bringing Hesiod's poems to modern ears.

Catherine M. Schlegel
University of Notre Dame
May 2006

TRANSLATOR'S INTRODUCTION

WHEN CATHERINE SCHLEGEL AND I FIRST DISCUSSED THE possibility of collaborating on a verse-translation of the *Works and Days,* her favorite poem in Greek, I was at first skeptical. Hesiod is a poet who is able to sing fluently in virtually every poetic register and move smoothly from register to register without any sense of strain: in one passage he invokes the Muses and in another he tells you how to make a plow or about his legal wrangles with his brother. Could all of this be done in the contemporary English of our day—that is, in a way that would allow Hesiod to sing and would thus make a difference to English poetry? What made this translation possible, and then deeply satisfying and exciting for me (a work that took over many of my days), was the discovery of a verse-form capacious enough to carry over the material contained in Hesiod's dactylic hexameter line and yet rigorous enough to allow for a technical struggle that could yield a lyricism of its own in translation. In the process of experimenting with various forms, I hit on iambic heptameter couplets, otherwise known, since the Renaissance, as *fourteeners.* This was the verse-form in which Arthur Golding's translation of Ovid's *Metamorphoses* (which Ezra

Pound called "the most beautiful book in English") had been rendered, as well as the one in which Chapman's Homer (or at least his *Iliad*—his *Odyssey* is in a much more nondescript blank verse) had found its way to Keats. The *fourteener* had fallen into desuetude over the years (over the last four hundred, as a matter of fact), but it seemed to me that by varying the position of the caesura, by loosening the meter through occasional anapests (as the matter required), and by sprinkling slant-rhymes in with straight ones, the *fourteener* could be modernized or revivified and made less rigid to the modern sensibility. I realize now in retrospect that I was looking for something strange and unfamiliar, a verse-form that could cut across the grain of the contemporary *patois* and by turns be both colloquial and archaic. If one were going to invoke the Muses or describe how to build a plow—in the English of the twenty-first century—there would have to be some formal *protection,* as it were, some way of lifting and distancing the language from the ordinary American idiom, that would enable one to suspend his disbelief: in the first case, because invoking the Muse seems too "poetic" to us now, and, in the second, because building a plow seems too "prosaic." Since the eighteenth century (but the process was already under way by then), the various poetic genres have been eaten up by prose, with the result that, by and large, the only genre remaining to poetry in our time is the "lyric"—which is to say, the short poem written in a free verse that might as well be called prose (except for line breaks that usually have no musical basis). Encompassing Hesiod's many registers in what passes for poetry in the contemporary scene would not be especially difficult, but, for that reason, not especially worth doing; the problem comes when one tries to put him into verse. Hesiod is an astonishing and very beautiful poet; but it seemed to me that he hadn't been heard in English, or at least not for a very long time. The *fourteeners* gave me a way to let him be heard.

The beauty of the English *fourteener* lies not only in its capaciousness but also in its flexibility. Iambic pentameter, the most common of English meters, a five-beat, ten-syllable line, which the eighteenth century referred to as English heroic verse, is simply too short to encompass the material contained in the dactylic hexameter of Greek epic poetry, a six-foot, eighteen-syllable line; for this reason, a translator who opts for iambic pentameter (as Dorothea Wender, in her fine, serviceable translation of Hesiod, does) will be obliged to forgo a line-by-line rendering and compose a translation that has many more lines than the original. Iambic hexameter, a six-beat, twelve-syllable line, has never been widely used, not even in the Renaissance, because it is too heavy and unwieldy for longer stretches: the caesura, or pause, always falls in the middle of the iambic hexameter line, after the sixth syllable, and thus the rhythm will tend to grow tedious after a time. The iambic heptameter line of the *fourteener* is both long enough to encompass the Greek and at the same time flexible enough to produce a good deal of rhythmic variation: the caesura usually falls after the fourth foot (or eighth syllable), but it can be made to fall after the third or even the fifth foot; in the latter case, something akin to internal enjambment occurs (enjambment being the running-over of one line into another without pause). Moreover, the caesura can be made to fall after the seventh syllable, which imparts a "feminine" quality to the pause (a feminine ending occurs when a line ends with an unaccented syllable), or even after the ninth or eleventh syllables. And since in *fourteeners* two lines are "coupled" by the rhyme, the symmetry of the form can either be emphasized or de-emphasized through metrical variation (I have made considerable use of anapestic rhythms, for example) and through the use of either true or slant rhyme.

Let me offer a few examples. In the following couplet, the first line conforms to the most typical situation, with the caesura falling after the fourth foot; but the second line has a trochaic substitution in the first foot (very common in iambic meter) and the caesura comes after the third foot:

> Poseidon who engirds the earth and shakes it far and wide,
> Themis who is revered and Aphrodite glancing-eyed.
>
> (*Th* 15–16)

In the first line of the following couplet, the caesura falls after the seventh syllable, and in the second there is a slight pause after the fourth and another after the eleventh syllable:

> And scattered out its contents, bringing humans grievous pain:
> And only hope in its unbroken dwelling did remain.
>
> (*WD* 95–96)

This "double-caesura" effect is not uncommon because of the length of the heptameter. In the following passage,

> And echoes in the homes of the immortals. The divine
> Singing that they send forth gives fame, first to the reverend line
> Of deathless ones whom Gaia bore to Ouranos—her brood
> And those that sprung from them are gods, givers of all things
>   good
>
> (*Th* 43–46),

the first line has pauses after the sixth and eleventh syllables, the second after the eighth syllable, the third after the fourth and twelfth syllables, and the fourth after the eighth syllable again. (The second line has trochaic substitutions in the first and fifth feet, and the fourth line in the fifth foot.)

One more example:

> The deathless ones, who dwell upon Olympos, as of old,
> In the beginning made a race of mortals that was gold.
> These people lived in Kronos' time, when he was heaven's king;
> Like gods they lived, with carefree heart, remote from suffering.
>   (*WD* 109–12)

Only the third line in this passage is altogether regular—that is, has the caesura after the fourth foot. The first line has pauses after the fourth and eleventh syllables, the second after the fifth and eleventh, and the fourth after the fourth as well as the eighth.

This translation will perhaps be criticized for its use of rhyme, given the fact that ancient Greek poetry has none. The obvious rejoinder to this is that though the translation is *of* an ancient Greek poem, it is being done *into* English and rhyme is one of the resources of English poetry. Milton, in the preface to *Paradise Lost,* wanted to restore to English the "ancient liberty" of the heroic poem and therefore polemicized against the "troublesome and modern bondage of Rhiming"; but we are now in a very different cultural situation, and if we are again in bondage it is now clearly to prose and to various "prosaic" tendencies that have infected poetry. Of course, rhyme is a necessary adjunct to the meter: *fourteeners* are in couplets because so long a line would become shapeless without the use of consecutive rhyme. Rhyme allows for a kind of linear *sculpting* that would otherwise be difficult to obtain. But, in addition, there was something specific to Hesiod's line that made me sense instinctively that rhyme would not only help to distance the language and lift it above its mundane uses but could also play a role in organizing the "controlled chaos" of Hesiod's syntax. Hesiod composes in very long sentences, with all kinds of syntactical leaps and with images and ideas flying in at odd angles. In a sentence such as the following one, for example (which has to do with Zeus's destruction of the monster Typhoeus), rhyme has the purpose, and I hope the effect, of modulating the free flow of Hesiod's energy in a way that neither restrains it nor allows it to become overly diffuse:

> Then, when he had subdued him by the strokes that he sent down,
> The crippled monster fell—gigantic Gaia gave a groan—
> And flame shot from the body of the thunder-stricken lord,

Till rugged Aetna's mountain slopes and valleys were devoured
And much of the prodigious earth was burned and wasted in
The preternatural fire's breath—melted, as is tin
When, in the well-aired crucible where craftsmen work their
    skill,
Heat softens it; or as is iron, strongest thing of all,
When subject to a fire burning in hilly vales, at length
It's melted in the sacred earth through great Hephaistos' strength.

(*Th* 857–68)

As this passage indicates, however, I have made rather full use in the translation of slant rhyme—i.e., rhyme in which the consonants of the rhyming syllables are the same but the vowel sounds are slightly different. "Down" and "groan" and "lord" and "devoured" are what one might call "true" slant rhymes (if that isn't too much of a contradiction), but if my ear has also been open to "skill" and "all" and to still more egregious examples in this translation, it is because I have wanted above all to preserve the free and spontaneous movement of Hesiod's versification while at the same time remaining as faithful as possible to what he had to say.

The versification and hence the final composition has been mine, but this translation has been a collaboration in the fullest sense. I am a poet and have done a fair amount of translation, mainly of French poetry, but I have only a little Greek and would never have undertaken anything so ambitious as a translation of Hesiod without the collaboration of a scholar such as Catherine Schlegel. Here is how our collaboration worked in practice. For every line of the Greek text, Professor Schlegel furnished me not only with a literal translation but with a full philological "work-up," complete with notes on everything that could possibly be of relevance, including textual difficulties, interpretive quandaries, and so on. I relied on her philological skills and on her deep understanding both of the historical context in which Hesiod wrote and of the scholarly tradition in terms of which he has been interpreted and edited. She worked with all of the available commentaries on Hesiod—in English, German, and other languages—and she very often acquainted me with details that I would never have recognized on my own. On the basis of the material that Professor Schlegel gave me, I constructed the verse. She evaluated what I had done, and, if necessary, I made changes in accordance with her comments. (It was irritating when, having spent hours putting a particular passage into verse, I learned that I had misconstrued something and would have to undo the thread of my labors and weave it over again!) I relied not only on her scholarly discretion but on her feeling for Hesiod's poetry and, very often, on her concrete word choices. It was a joy to work with her, and so meticulous was she that I think that her work was harder and more time-consuming than my own.

This translation was certainly a labor of love for both of us, and now, having completed it, we can only hope that it will give pleasure to readers and perhaps even open up a poetic world of which they were previously unaware.

Henry Weinfield
University of Notre Dame
May 2006

A NOTE ON
PRONUNCIATION
AND SPELLING

THIS TRANSLATION FOLLOWS THE TEXT OF M. L. WEST'S *Oxford Classical Text.* We have preserved the line-number irregularities that occur in the Greek text. These are a result of what scholars recognize to be flaws in the transmission of the text. Line 111 of the *Theogony,* for example, is missing, and the numbering goes from line 110 to 112; what had come down in the textual tradition as line 111 was a repetition of line 46 and so has been judged by editors to have been mistakenly introduced into the text by some accident of time or copying.

In the transliteration of Greek names, we have generally tried to follow the Greek pronunciation and orthography rather than the Latin equivalent; thus, Akhilleus rather than Achilles. Greek names are often familiar in their Latinized versions, however, and therefore we thought that it would be better to retain the familiar spellings in some cases than to preserve complete consistency. Thus, Helicon is given with the Latinate "c" rather than the Greek "k." But because this is a poetic translation, tonal and rhythmic considerations have taken precedence; thus, Akhilleus rather than Achilles, even though the latter is the more familiar form.

A word on possessives ending in "s": if the possessive creates an extra syllable, is pronounced, and takes up a position in the meter—for example, if "Zeus's" sounds as two syllables—then an additional "s" is added in the text, as in *Theogony,* line 13: "And of Athena, aegis-bearing Zeus's gray-eyed daughter." If the syllable indicating the possessive is not pronounced, or pronounced only slightly, and adds no syllable to the meter, then no extra "s" is added in the text. An example is *Theogony,* line 793: "For if one of the gods who hold Olympos' snowy peak."

We have included a detailed guide for the pronunciation of Greek names with the glossary at the back.

THEOGONY

THEOGONY

From the Heliconian Muses, let us now begin the song
Of those who hold the great and sacred hill of Helicon,
And dance on tender feet around the dark spring in a row,
And round about the altar of the son of Kronos go;
5   And when in the Permessos they have bathèd their soft, young skin,
Or sacred stream Olmeios or the fountain Hippocrene,
They make their dancing chorus on the heights of Helicon—
So beautiful, beguiling, as their feet glide swiftly on.
Then afterwards they rise up and they venture forth by night,
10   Wrapped in deep mist and uttering sweet sound that gives delight,
To sing of aegis-bearing Zeus and also of his queen,
Hera of Argos, she who wears the sandals of gold sheen,
And of Athena, aegis-bearing Zeus's gray-eyed daughter,
Phoebus Apollo, Artemis as well, the arrow shooter,
15   Poseidon who engirds the earth and shakes it far and wide,
Themis who is revered and Aphrodite glancing-eyed,
And Hebe golden-garlanded, lovely Dione and
Leto and Iapetos, Kronos of crooked mind,
And Eos and great Helios, Selena shining bright,

20 Gaia (the Earth) and Okeanos (Ocean), Nux (the Night),
And all the other deathless ones, eternal in their breed.

The Muses once to Hesiod taught lovely song indeed,
While he was tending to his sheep on holy Helicon;
And this is what those goddesses first to me made known,
25 The Muses of Olympos, maids of aegis-bearing Zeus:
"You shepherds of the wilderness, mere bellies, poor excuse
For men, we can make falsities and fallacies seem true,
But when we want we're able to give truthful statements too."
The ready-spoken daughters of great Zeus had this to say,
30 And gave me a staff that they had plucked, a branch of flowering bay,
A wondrous thing! and breathed a god-inspired voice in me,
That I might celebrate the things that were and that shall be;
And bade me hymn the race of those who always are, the blessed,
But make my song be always of themselves, both first and last.
35 But why all this concerning tree or rock? Come, let's begin
With the Muses, who to Zeus the father when they sing
Give pleasure to his mighty mind, telling of things that are,
Of things in future that shall be, and things that were before.
Out of their mouths in sweet, unwearying harmony the voice
40 Flows, and the halls of Father Zeus the thunderer rejoice
At the subtle music of those goddesses; the sound
Causes the snowy summits of Olympos to resound
And echoes in the homes of the immortals. The divine
Singing that they send forth gives fame, first to the reverend line
45 Of deathless ones whom Gaia bore to Ouranos: her brood
46 And those that sprung from them are gods, givers of all things good.
47 Then secondly they sing of Zeus, father of gods and men,
49 The most courageous of the gods and mightiest; and then,
50 In turn, of human beings and of giants of great might,
And to the mind of Zeus upon Olympos give delight,
The Muses of Olympos, of the aegis-bearing one.

Mnemosyne in Pieria, unto the Kronion,
Bore them to be forgetfulness and rest from cares and ills;
55 She was the guardian goddess of the Eleutherian hills,
And Zeus the all-wise counselor for nine nights lay with her:
He went up to her holy bed when the gods were nowhere near.
So when in time the seasons turned and the months began to wane,
When the year had been accomplished and had cycled back again,
60 She bore nine daughters—girls of but one thought, whose hearts' sole care
Was song, and in their souls sorrow would never have a share—
Near to Olympos's highest snow-capped peak; she bore them there,
And there their lovely dwellings and their shining dance floors are,
And near them, joined in feasting, are the Graces and Desire.
65 And when they sing the customs, cherished manners that belong
Unto the deathless ones, whom they make glorious by their song,
Delightful is the charming sound that through their lips is sent.
The Muses, with immortal song, once to Olympos went,
Glorying in their lovely voice; the black earth all around
70 Rang with their singing; from beneath their pulsing feet the sound
Rose as they went up to their father—he, being heaven's king,
Himself keeps hold of thunder and the blazing lightning,
Having by conquest overcome his father, Kronos, and
Given the deathless ones fair laws, honors and ranks ordained.
75 The Olympian Muses sang these things and, singing, made them known,
The nine daughters born to mighty Zeus the Kronion:
Clio, Euterpe, Thalia, Erato, Melpomene,
Urania, Polyhymnia, also Terpsichore,
And finally Calliope—and she is most preferred,
80 For she attends on kings who have a claim to be revered.
And if the daughters of great Zeus should recognize the worth
Of one whom Zeus has cherished and should look upon his birth,
They pour sweet dew upon his tongue, and then the words will stream
Out of his mouth like honey, and people will look to him

Theogony

85 As one who can distinguish with straight justice what should be;
   And he in the assembly hall, who speaks unerringly,
   Even has expertise to quell great quarrels in good season.
   (This is the reason there are prudent kings, and for this reason
   When people have been wronged, fair restitution can be made
90 Easily, for with calming words their arguments persuade.)
   When he goes to the assembly hall, they treat him like a god,
   With reverence, and he stands out distinct among the crowd.
   Such is the Muses' sacred gift to humankind; for through
   The Muses and Apollo the far shooter it is so
95 That there are singers on the earth and harpers that exist;
   Though rulers are from Zeus, the one the Muses love is blessed,
   And sweet the song that flows out from his mouth; for even though
   A man whose spirit anguishes with freshly piercing woe
   Be dried up in his breast from weeping, should a singer then,
100 A servant of the Muses, sing the fame of ancient men
   And of the blessèd gods who dwell on Mount Olympos, soon
   This man will cease remembering the sorrow he has known,
   Diverted by the gods' gifts from his sadness speedily.
       Hail, daughters of Zeus, and may you grant delightful song to me,
105 That I may hymn the sacred race of those who never die,
   They who were born of Gaia (Earth), Ouranos (starry Sky),
   And Nux (the dusky Night) as well as Pontos (the salt Sea).
   Say firstly how the first ones, gods and Earth, first came to be,
   And rivers and unbounded ocean with its furious swell,
110 And the shining stars and broad firmament over all,
112 And how they shared the riches and the honors that then followed,
113 And how they took possession of Olympos many-hollowed.
114 Speak all these things, Muses, from your high Olympian home:
115 From the beginning, tell me which of these was first to come.
       Chasm it was, in truth, who was the very first; she soon
   Was followed by broad-breasted Earth, the eternal ground of all

The deathless ones, who on Olympos's snowy summits dwell,
And murky Tartaros hidden deep from Earth's wide-open roads,
120 And Eros, the most beautiful among the deathless gods—
Limb-loosener he is of all the gods and of all men:
Thought in the breast he overwhelms and prudent planning; then
Out of Chasm Erebos and black Night both were born,
And then from Night came Ether and came Day as well in turn;
125 For Night conceived them, having joined with Erebos in love.
Now Earth first brought forth Ouranos, the starry Sky above,
An equal to herself, so he could cover her around,
And she might serve the deathless gods as firm, eternal ground.
She bore the hills, the gracious haunts of mountain goddesses then—
130 The Nymphs, who range the wooded hills and up and down each glen;
And without sweet desiring love, she bore the barren Sea,
Pontos, the raging salt-sea swell; and when she had lain with Sky,
She bore deep-eddying Ocean and Koios and Kreios too,
Hyperion, father of the Sun, Iapetos also,
135 And Thea and Rhea and Themis and, in turn, Mnemosyne,
Phoebe the golden-crownèd one, Tethys lovely to see;
And after these the youngest came, Kronos, crooked and sly,
The cleverest of all her children and his father's enemy.
        And, further, the Kyklopes with their wanton hearts she bore—
140 Brontes, Steropes, Arges: Thunder, Flash, quick-striking Power—
Who gave Zeus thunder and who wrought the thunderbolt. Whereas
They were a good deal like the gods in many other ways,
In the middle of their foreheads each one had a single eye—
And hence the name Kyklopes, which means "circle eyes," you see;
145 For each one had a rounded eye in the middle of his head.
Muscular strength and skill were in their works and all they did.
        From Gaia and from Ouranos these others also came—
Three huge and mighty children, whom one even dreads to name:
Kottos, Briareos, Gyges—haughty sons with monstrous forms;

150 For from their shoulders each of them sprouted a hundred arms,
And from each sturdy shoulder fifty heads, ungainly, grew
And sat upon his massive limbs, and each one of this crew
Had endless strength of body in his huge, misshapen girth.
    Now of the many children that were born to Sky and Earth,
155 These were the fiercest ones, and from the very outset they
Were hated by their father and he hid them all away,
As soon as they were born, deep in the earth; he took delight
In doing this wicked deed and did not let them reach the light.
But Gaia, thronging inwardly, prodigious, gave a groan,
160 And she devised a crafty piece of cunning of her own.
She made a kind of metal that was gray and very hard,
Fashioned a scythe and showed her children what she had prepared;
And though she grieved in her own heart, to make them bold she said:
"O children, born to me and of a father who is bad,
165 We'll take an evil vengeance on him, if you should agree:
If anyone was first to do things shameful, it was he."
    She spoke thus, but fear gripped them; not a single word resounded—
Till great and wily Kronos, taking courage, thus responded
In speech addressing his dear mother: "Mother, I promise you,
170 I'll take this task upon myself and do what I must do.
I do not scruple about our ill-named father; for as you see,
If anyone was first to do things shameful, it was he."
    He finished, and gigantic Gaia's heart with joy expands.
She hides him in an ambush and she places in his hands
175 A saw-toothed sickle and explains the cunning stratagem.
    Great Ouranos came bringing on the night, and as he came
He lay outstretched on Gaia in his longing to make love—
And then his son in ambush reached his left hand out and drove
The sickle with his right hand (it was toothed and of great length),
180 And hacked his father's genitalia off with all his strength.
Impetuously he reaped them; then he threw them out behind

Him backwards; nor did they fly off fruitless to the wind;
For each one of the bloody drops that flew away soon found
Its path to Earth and was received; and when the year came round,

185　She bore the Furies (Erinyes) and Giants of great might
(They bear long spears; their armor and their weaponry shine bright),
And bore the Nymphs, the Meliai, as they on earth are called.
As soon as with the adamantine metal he had culled
The genitals, he threw them out into the surging main:

190　There on the waves they rose and fell and rose and fell again;
And round about the immortal flesh white foam arose, and from
That foam a girl was born—she first to Kythera did come,
To sacred Kythera, and thence to sea-girt Kypris came,
And stepped upon the shore a lovely goddess with a claim

195　To reverence, and grass sprang up beneath her feet; her name
Is Aphrodite—gods and men both call her this (since from
The *aphros* she was nurtured—yes, within the frothy foam),
And also Kytherea, since from Kythera she was come,
And Kyprogenia, having been on sea-washed Kypris born,

200　And laughter loving, coming from the members that were torn.
Eros walked beside her; lovely Longing close behind
Followed as soon as she was born and also when she joined
The gods' race; and this honor, from the first, was hers on high—
This portion among human beings and the gods who never die:

205　Fond and familiar talk of girls and pleasure's sweet caress,
Smiles and deceptions, honeyed love, kindness, gentleness.
　　　As for this strain of progeny, great Ouranos, complaining,
Called them Titans (Strainers) on account of all their straining.
Without restraint in wickedness they'd strained to do the deed,

210　But would be recompensed in time for what they'd done, he said.
211　　　Then Night gave birth to dreadful Doom, black Bane, these two,
　　　and more—
212　Mortality; then Sleep, and then the race of Dreams she bore;

214 Then Ridicule and grievous Woe (although she had not lain

213 With any of the deathless gods) dark Night brought forth; and then

215 The Hesperides, who far beyond famed Okeanos dwell—

216 They tend the golden apples and the apple trees as well;

217 And both the Moirai and the ruthless goddesses of Bane,

220 Who track the deviations and the crimes of gods and men,

Nor ever is their dreadful wrath abated till they serve

Harsh vengeance on the evildoer, such as he may deserve.

Then fatal Night bore Nemesis, a bane to men who die,

And after that Deception and Affectionate Intimacy;

225 And cursed, destructive Age and Strife steel-hearted bore she then.

Then hateful Strife gave birth to Toil, bringer of grievous pain,

To Famine and Oblivion and to Sorrows that cause tears,

Combats, Contentions, Murders, and Slaughter-of-Men-in-Wars,

To Quarrels, Lies, and Arguments, Disputes of every feature,

230 To Lawlessness and Recklessness that share a common nature;

And Oath, who most of all does harm to men that are earth-born,

Whenever someone by his own free will has falsely sworn.

Then Pontos fathered Nereus—this was his eldest son:

Old man Nereus, so called because that truthful one

235 Makes *nary an error:* he is kind and worthy of all trust,

Does not forget the righteous ways, and knows which plans are just;

And then in turn by mingling with Gaia he begat

Heroic Phorkys, fair-cheeked Keto, Thaumas, who is great,

And Eurybia, whose spirit in her breast is adamant.

240 Many goddess children in the barren sea were sent

To Nereus and to Doris of the lovely hair (she came

As daughter of circling Okeanos, never-ending stream):

Protho and Eukrante, also Sao and Amphitrite,

Eudora and then Thetis next, Galena and then Glauke,

245 Kymothoë and swift Speio, also Thalia full of charms,

Erato, Pasithea, and Eunike with rosy arms,

Melita of many graces and Agave and Eulimine,
Doto, Proto, Pherousa, in addition to Dynamene,
Nesaea and Actaea and Protomedea too,
250   Beautiful Galatea, Doris, Panope also,
And lovely Hippothoë and rose-armed Hipponoë,
And Kymodoke, she who soothes the swollen, misty sea;
Along with Kymatolege and trim-ankled Amphitrite
She soothes the blasts of the blowing gusts—she does it easily;
255   Then Kymo and Eione and garlanded Halimede,
Pontoporea also, laughter-loving Glaukonome,
Leagore, Euagore as well, Laomedea,
Poulynoë, Autonoë, and then Lysianassa;
With lovely mien and shapely form, Euarne; then Psamathe,
260   With charming body full of grace; also divine Menippe,
Eupompe, Neso, Pronoë, Themisto, and refined
Nemertes, who is like her deathless father in her mind.
These were the fifty daughters blameless Nereus was sent:
They practiced various blameless arts; their skills were excellent.
265   Now Thaumas wed Elektra, child to brimming Okeanos,
And she gave birth in time to a swift-footed daughter, Iris,
To Okypete and Aiello, harpies with lovely hair,
Who follow along the swooping blasts—on speeding wings they soar;
On speeding wings they track the winds, flying up high in air.
270   Then Keto bore to Phorkys the Old Women who are fair-
Cheeked with lovely faces and, being gray-haired from their birth,
Are called the Graiai by the gods and men who walk on earth:
Fine-robed Pemphredo and golden-robed Enyo; and then as well,
She bore the Gorgons, who far beyond famed Okeanos dwell
275   At the edge of night (where the clear-voiced Hesperides dwell also):
Sthenno and Euryale, Medusa who suffered woe,
Being mortal, while the other two could neither age nor die;
But only with Medusa did the dark-haired sea god lie

Down in a meadow of spring flowers, on a soft and grassy bed.
280 And so when Perseus cut her off by cutting off her head,
Out sprang Chrysaor and then sprang out Pegasus the horse:
The *pegai* (springs) whence Pegasus sprang were near to Ocean's source,
And the golden sword (*aor chryseion*) gave Chrysaor his name.
Then Pegasus forsook the earth, mother of flocks, and came
285 To dwell within the halls of Zeus among the gods and bring
Unto the all-wise counselor thunder and lightning.
Chrysaor fathered Geryon meanwhile, the triple-headed—
It was the maid Kallirhoë, great Ocean's child, he bedded;
But Geryon was killed by mighty Herakles in battle
290 In sea-swept Erytheia near the shambling, broad-browed cattle,
Which he to sacred Tiryns on that day was driving on;
And having crossed the narrow straits of Ocean, he cut down
Eurytion the cowherd and Orthos the dog as well—
In the murky farmstead out beyond the salt sea-swell.
295   Then in a hollow cave she bore another monstrous creature—
Impossible, not like the gods or mortals in its nature:
This was the fierce Echidna, a divine and dauntless maid;
And half she was a lovely girl, fair-cheeked and glancing-eyed,
And half a serpent, terrible, prodigious in its girth,
300 Eating raw flesh and slithering in the depths of sacred earth.
There in a hollow, rocky place, deep down, she had a den,
Far away from the deathless gods and far away from men:
Such was the fabled dwelling that the gods for her decreed.
    In the land of the Arimoi, beneath the earth, she stayed—
305 Baleful Echidna—all her days an ageless, deathless maid.
But Typhon mingled with her in love—or so it has been said,
The terrible, unruly one with her of the glancing eye;
So she conceived and she gave birth to dauntless progeny.
Orthos, a dog for Geryon—this was the first she bore;
310 Then one that was impossible, unspeakable, the cur

Kerberos of Hades, fifty-headed, with great power:
Shameless, he had a brazen voice and raw flesh would devour.
The baleful-hearted Hydra was the one that she bore third—
Hydra of Lerna, whom the white-armed goddess Hera reared
315 To wreak her wrath on Herakles—but Herakles, the son
Of both Amphitryon and Zeus, slaughtered that monstrous one
With help from Iolaus who loves Ares (it was planned
By Athena who rules the war hosts and was at her high command).

But she bore the fierce Chimaera, who breathes overwhelming fire;
320 Huge, mighty, and fleet footed, she is terrible and dire.
321 She had three heads, the Chimaera: first a lion that would glower,
322 Then the second was a she-goat, last a serpent of great power.
325 Bellerophon and Pegasus despatched her; even so,
She bore the Sphinx (who brought the house of Kadmos death and woe)
When Orthos had subdued her, the Nemean lion too,
Which Hera, Zeus's glorious mate, nurtured until it grew,
Then settled in the Nemean hills—for humankind a bane:
330 So, living there it brought destruction to the tribes of men,
Ruling Nemean Tretos and the Apesas ruling too;
But the sheer force of Heraklean power laid it low.

Now Keto, having lain with Phorkys, brought her last-born forth,
A fearsome snake, who deep in the vast chambers of black earth
335 Guards within its boundaries the apples of pure gold—
And thus the race of Keto and of Phorkys has been told.

These are the whirling rivers that Tethys to Ocean bore:
The Nile, the Alph, the Eridanos eddying with a roar,
The Strymon and Maeander and the Ister's lovely flow,
340 The Phasis, Rhesus, silver-swirling Acheloüs too,
The Nessus, Rhodius, Haliakmon, and the Heptaporus,
Granikos and the marvelous Simois, the Aesepus,
The Peneus, the Hermus, the fair-flowing Kaikos, and
The Ladon, the Parthenius, Sangarius so grand,

345 Euenus and Aldeskos and the wondrous Scamander.

       Then Tethys bore the holy race of Maidens, nymphs who wander

Over the earth, and with Apollo and the rivers raise

Men up to manhood—this is their role, the one that Zeus decrees:

Admete and Ianthe and Elektra, also Peitho,

350 Divinely formed Urania, in addition, Doris, Prymno,

Hippo and Klymene and Rhodeia and Kallirhoë,

And Zeuxo and Klytia and Idyia and Pasithoë,

Dione, the enticing, and Plexaura, Galaxaura,

Theo and Melobosis and the beautiful Polydora,

355 Perseis, Ianeira, and Kerkeis of noble size,

Akaste, yes, and Xanthe too, Pluto with great wide eyes,

Desirable Petraia and Europa and Menestho,

And Metis and Eurynome and yellow-veiled Telestho,

Asia as well as Chrysis, with the arousing one, Kalypso,

360 Eudora, Tyche, Amphirho, Okyrhoë, Styx also—

Styx, who is most excelling, plainly first of all of them.

       These are the first-born daughters that to Ocean and Tethys came;

But there are many more—with names that cannot be rehearsed:

Three thousand of the trim-legged Okeanids are dispersed,

365 And far and wide across the earth and deep within the sea

These shining children of the gods are scattered equally;

But just as many rivers flow, resounding with a roar,

The sons of Okeanos, whom the queenly Tethys bore;

And though no single mortal man can utter each one's name,

370 Their names are known to everyone who lives nearby to them.

       Then Thea bore great Helios, Selena shining bright,

And Eos, the Dawn, who unto all the things of earth brings light,

To all the things of earth and to the gods who hold the sky—

Thea unto Hyperion brought forth this progeny.

375 Then Eurybia mixed in love with Kreios; she, divine,

Gave birth to Pallas and great Astraios; also in her line

Was Perses—he who stands apart for wisdom and for skill.
Then Eos with Astraios bore the mighty winds: the chill,
Swift-speeding north wind Boreas, the west wind Zephyros,
380 Notos the south wind—Eos lulled in love lay languorous;
And after these the child of morn brought forth Eosphoros,
The Morning Star, and all the stars that circle over us.

      Now Styx, the daughter of Ocean, mixed with Pallas; she gave birth
To lovely-ankled Victory and Glory, then brought forth
385 Power and Strength her children, both of them illustrious:
They have no separate dwelling nor a place apart from Zeus,
Nor any motivation save where Zeus directs their road,
But always they sit near to him, the heavy-thundering god.
For so the daughter of Ocean, everlasting Styx, had planned
390 Upon that day on which the Olympian lightener gave command
That all the immortal gods should come to Olympos's lofty height;
For whosoever, so he said, among the gods should fight
Against the Titans by his side would have no loss of fame
Or any rights among the gods which he was wont to claim;
395 And anyone who under Kronos was without esteem,
Prizes and privilege, as is right, he would bestow on him.
And so it was that Styx, the everlasting one, first came
To Olympos with her children—her dear father hatched the scheme.
Zeus gave her honor and he gave prodigious gifts to her,
400 And made her the great oath by which the Olympian gods all swear,
Decreeing that her children should dwell with him for all days;
And everything he promised he fulfilled in all these ways,
For he himself is master and is powerful indeed.

      And then, in turn, came Phoebe to the sweet-delighting bed
405 Of Koios, and conceiving through the god's embrace a child
She bore dark-veilèd Leto, who is always kind and mild
As well to human beings as to the never-dying gods—
From the beginning gentlest in the Olympian abodes.

Phoebe gave birth to honored Asteria then, the spouse
410 In later time of Perses when he brought her to his house;
And she gave birth to Hekate, who more than anyone
Was honored and given splendid gifts by Zeus the Kronion—
Having a portion of the earth and of the barren sea,
And of the starry sky as well an honored share; and she
415 Is honored most of all among the deathless gods; for, still,
Whenever someone on the earth where human beings dwell
Is offering sacred sacrifices in the proper way,
If he should call on Hekate, honor and dignity
Will easily attend on him—if she should hear his prayer:
420 She'll even grant him happiness—this is within her power.
For of the many children that Earth unto Sky did bear,
All with a sphere of influence, of each she has a share;
And never did the son of Kronos take away the honor
Which, when the Titans ruled of old, had been conferred upon her,
425 But still she holds her portion as it was in the beginning;
426 And though she was an only child, there was no undermining
427 Of what was given her on earth and in the sky and sea:
428 Because Zeus gives her honor she has yet much more; and he
429 Whom she has chosen to support has many benefits:
434 When judgments are being handed down, with reverend kings she sits;
430 And whom in the assembly she has chosen none ignore;
431 And also when men arm themselves for death-delivering war,
432 The goddess stands near those to whom she grants the victory,
433 Gladly bestowing glory and renown by her decree.
439   She is a boon to horsemen when she wants to stand near them,
435 A boon as well to athletes seeking prizes in a game:
436 The goddess stands nearby, conferring benefits on these;
437 And when by force and strength a man has won, the lovely prize
438 Is carried off in gladness and his parents reap renown.
440 Also for those who toil on stormy seas she is a boon—

Who pray to the loud Earth-Shaker and to Hekate as well:
To these the glorious goddess grants full quarry, if she will,
But steals it away, if that should please her heart, when it's in view.
She is a boon, along with Hermes, on the farmstead too,
445 Fostering herds of cattle and broad herds of goats also,
And flocks of sheep with wooly fleece, if she should wish it so:
From few she conjures many and from many she makes few.
And though she is the only child that her mother bore,
All honors among the deathless gods are given in gift to her.
450 The son of Kronos charged her with rearing children from that time on,
Soon as they'd seen the light with their eyes of the all-seeing Dawn.
Thus, from the first, she fosters them; these honors are all her own.

    When Rhea had been subdued by Kronos, she bore a glorious brood:
Hestia and Demeter and then Hera golden-shod,
455 And stalwart, ruthless Hades, he who dwells beneath the ground;
Also she bore the Shaker-of-Earth, who shakes it with loud sound,
And cunning Zeus, the father of the gods and mortals too,
Who with his thunder makes the broad earth tremble and quake also.
But these the mighty Kronos swallowed up as soon as from
460 Out of their mother's holy womb each toward her knees would come,
Deeming that no one else but he, of those who dwell on high,
Should hold the rank of king among the gods who never die;
For he had learned from Gaia and from starry Ouranos
That his own child would conquer him, powerful though he was—
465 And this was bound to happen through the plan of mighty Zeus.
Therefore he wasn't blind but keenly watched against the morrow—
And swallowed up his children, giving Rhea endless sorrow.

    Now when she was about to bear the father of gods and men,
Zeus, she begged her own—her very own—dear parents then,
470 Gaia and starry Ouranos, to help her make a plan
So that she might give birth unseen to her belovèd son
And thus avenge the furies of her father—and each one

Of all those children whom the wily Kronos swallowed down.
They listened to their much belovèd daughter and gave heed,
475 And showed her what had been foretold to happen, as she bade,
To what had been foretold for Kronos and his strong-souled son.
So when she was about to bear great Zeus, her youngest one,
They sent her off to Lyktos, to the fertile land of Crete.
Prodigious Gaia took this child that Rhea did beget,
480 To cherish and to foster him in Crete, the wide-spaced land.
She brought him through the fleet, dark night till Lyktos was at hand,
Then taking him within her arms she hid him underground
Within the depths of sacred earth in a sheer, dark cave she found
Beneath the Aegean mountain where thick stands of trees abound.
485 But to the son of Ouranos, the older gods' great lord,
A huge rock wrapped in swaddling clothes she gave to be devoured.
He took it in his hand and in his belly crammed it down,
Not knowing that he'd swallowed rock, the brute, and that his son
Was left behind unconquered and unharmed—that very soon
490 He would be overwhelmed by force, abandoned, overthrown,
Deprived of status and his son made ruler in his place.
        Now swiftly did the prowess of the master then increase;
His glorious limbs assumed their strength; and with the cycling year,
Kronos, through Gaia's shrewd suggestion, fell into the snare:
495 He vomited out his offspring, did great Kronos of crooked wit,
Defeated by the strength and skill of him whom he begat;
And first he vomited up the stone, since last he gulped it down:
Zeus fixed it firm upon the broad-pathed earth and set it on
Holy Pytho, under Parnassus, in a hollow glen
500 To be a sign hereafter, a marvel for death-born men.
        He freed the sons of Ouranos, his father's brothers, from
The deadly chains with which their foolish father shackled them.
They recompensed the favor of this kindness with the crash-
ing thunder, smoking thunderbolt, and blazing lightning flash,

505 Which Gaia the prodigious had kept hidden until then:
With these things to support him, he rules over gods and men.

     Klymene, a slender-ankled maid of Okeanos, wed
Iapetos: he took her and he led her to their bed.
To him she bore stout Atlas, a strong souled and mighty son,
510 Renowned Menoitios, brilliant Prometheus, the clever, shifty one,
And Epimetheus, the mind that missed the mark—from whom,
For men who labor for their bread, evil was first to come;
For he received the molded girl from Zeus into his home.
The violent Menoitios far-seeing Zeus flung down
515 To darkness with a thunderbolt, by reason of his own
Arrogance and insolence, virile presumption.

     Now Atlas, by compulsion, holds the broad sky in his hands:
Near the clear-voiced Hesperides, at the bounds of earth, he stands,
And on his tireless shoulders and his head he props up heaven—
520 This is his lot, which Zeus the clever counselor has given.

     With breakless, grievous chains he bound Prometheus, then drove
Those chains into a pillar's midst so that he couldn't move,
And set a broad-winged eagle on the wily one: it flew
Down to eat his deathless liver, which always nightly grew
525 Back from what the broad-winged bird that day had swallowed down.
But mighty Herakles, at length, trim-legged Alkmene's son,
Destroyed it, thereby driving off that foul affliction,
Freeing the son of Iapetos from the miseries he had known—
And not without the will of Zeus, of him who rules on high,
530 So that the fame of Herakles, the Theban-born, should be
Greater upon the fruitful earth than in the days gone by.
Thus he revered his much renownèd son; and this is why,
Although he was enraged, he curbed his anger at the one
Who, in his scheming, strove against the mighty Kronion.

535   For at Mekone, when a pact between the gods and men
Was being struck, Prometheus, having a willful plan,

Apportioned an enormous ox and laid it out so that
He would deceive the mind of Zeus. Flesh, entrails rich in fat,
He hid them in the ox's tripe, sewn up in a hide;
540 The white bones of the ox he set by contrast to the side,
Hidden within the glistening fat—such was his crafty scheme.
And then the father of gods and mortals spoke, addressing him:
"Son of Iapetos, dear friend, renowned above all peers,
With what unfairness you have made division of the shares."
545 So Zeus, who knows unfailing counsels, taunting him, spoke thus.
And then addressing him in turn, wily Prometheus,
Bearing in mind his trick and slightly smirking, made reply:
"Great, glorious Zeus, most honored of the gods who never die,
Take which of these the spirit in your breast the better deems."
550 Duplicitously he spoke; but Zeus, who knows unfailing schemes,
Easily saw through the trick and in his mind beheld
Evils to come for mortal men, which soon would be fulfilled.
Then he took up in both his hands the white fat, and his breast
Was filled with anger—anger through his spirit swiftly passed
555 When he had seen how craftily the white bones had been placed.
And therefore, for the immortal ones, the various tribes of men
Have kindled on the smoking altars white ox bones since then.
　　　Then the Cloud-Gatherer in rage addressed Prometheus:
"Your schemes surpass all other schemes, son of Iapetos:
560 I see you haven't yet forgotten all your tricks, dear friend."
So Zeus spoke in his anger—he whose cunning has no end;
And ever recalling from that time the trick and his great ire,
He would not give to ash trees the unwearying force of fire
For death-born humans, they that dwell upon the earth; but Zeus
565 Was tricked completely by the brave Prometheus's bold ruse
When in a hollow fennel stalk he stole the far-seen glow
Of the unwearying force of fire—and that bit deep into
The heart within the thunderer's breast, provoking rage in him

When among human beings he saw the far-seen fire's gleam.
570   Then, for the price of fire, he made an evil for mankind,
Which from the earth Hephaistos, the famed Dextrous One, designed,
At Kronos's son's command, to be in likeness of a maid.
In shining silver raiment she was girded and arrayed
By Athena of the gray eyes, who drew down over her head
575 A hand-embroidered veil, which was a wondrous sight indeed;
578 And on her head the gray-eyed goddess placed a golden crown,
579 Which the far-famed Dextrous One created on his own,
580 Making the work by hand to please the mind of Zeus. Thereon,
Engraved with endless cunning, were things marvelous to see:
As many dire beasts as are on land and teem within the sea
He placed upon it, breathing on them all a charming grace—
Marvelous, like living things and things that have a voice.
585   The lovely evil he had made to countervail the good
He led out to the very spot where gods and mortals stood,
She glorious in the finery that she of the mighty father
Had given her—and wonder seized immortals and men together
When they had seen the steep, resistless snare befalling man.
590 From her the tribe of women comes—for men a grievous bane,
592 No helpmeets to their husbands when confronting Poverty,
593 But only their companions amid full Satiety.
594 So is it as in vaulted hives when bees feed lazy drones
595 (Who in their wicked deeds of sloth are boon companions),
And all day long until the sun is setting will not shirk
From laying down white honeycombs, attentive to their work:
The drones, by contrast, stay within the sheltered hives and gather
Into their stomachs all the work expended by another;
600 So in this way the Thunderer set out for mortal men
The woe that comes from women who conspire to bring men pain,
And gave another evil that would countervail the good:
If, fleeing from the baneful deeds of women, someone should

Prefer not to be married, then to dread senectitude

605 He'll come—without a soul to take care of his livelihood,
And when he's dead his kinsmen will divide his property.
Now, he who has a share in marriage as his destiny,
And has been joined together with a wise, devoted wife,
Even for him unwavering ill is measured all his life

610 Against the good; but should he be given the baneful sort,
Then unabating sorrow while he lives is in his heart,
And in his mind and spirit, and his heartache can't be healed.
It isn't possible to evade or hide what Zeus has willed.
Prometheus, Iapetos's guileless son, could never

615 Escape from Zeus's darkened rage, although he was so clever,
But rather by Necessity the great chain binds him down.

　　　When Ouranos in his spirit first felt anger at his son
Briareos, at Kottos and at Gyges also, he
Bound them in chains, indignant at their proud virility

620 And massive strength: he made them dwell beneath the broad-pathed earth,
And there, beneath its farthest edge, these children of great girth
Sat idle for a long, long while, and much did they complain,
Feeling great anguish in their hearts, immense anguish and pain.
But Zeus, the son of Kronos, and the other gods, whom bright-

625 Haired Rhea bore to Kronos, brought them back up to the light,
626 Prompted by Gaia's cunning; for she told them the whole story,
627 Saying that with the help of these three children they'd win glory
628 And carry off the conquest, splendid object of their prayers.
629 The spirit-grieving toil of doing battle had been theirs,
631 And they had fought fierce combats for too long against each other—
630 The Titan gods and those who had great Kronos for a father.
632 These, from lofty Othrys, were the Titans of great fame,
633 And those, the givers of all things good, from high Olympos came,
634 Whom bright-haired Rhea, having joined in love with Kronos, bore.
635 For ten full years continuously they now had been at war

In spirit-grieving battle, and there hadn't been release—
For either side—from bitter struggle; never did it ever cease:
The outcome was drawn evenly between them both. But when
Zeus had supplied these brothers with whatever might sustain
640 Them—nectar and ambrosia, on which the immortals feast—
641 And when the heroic spirit in their breasts had been increased,
643 The father of men and deathless gods addressed them, speaking thus:
644 "Hear me, shining children of Gaia and Ouranos,
645 That I may speak the things the heart within me bids me say.
For victory and mastery we struggle every day,
And it has been a long, long time we've fought against each other,
The Titan gods and we who have great Kronos for a father.
Now make known to the Titans your resistless arms, vast force,
650 As you oppose them in the grievous battle's mournful course,
Remembering our kind friendship and how many were your pains
Before you had reached the light once more, loosed from your cruel chains
And from the gloomy darkness through the actions that we took."

He finished; then at once replying, blameless Kottos spoke:
655 "The things that you have spoken of, dear sir, we know them well:
We know how much in thought and understanding you excel,
And how you've been a bulwark against ruin for the gods,
And, by your thoughtful wisdom, how you freed us from the abodes
Of gloomy darkness where we had been cruelly enchained:
660 What we could not have hoped for, son of Kronos, we have gained
Because of this. With stubborn minds and eager hearts, therefore,
We shall preserve your power and rule in the grim strife of war,
Fighting against the Titans in fierce combat." Thus he ended:
What they had heard the immortal givers of all good things commended;
665 And more than it had before, within their breasts the spirit burned
For war; and so they stirred the hated battle for which they yearned—
All of them, male and female, did on that decisive day:
The Titans and the gods who were of Kronos born—and they,

The ones whom Zeus from darkness under ground sent up to light,

670 And insolent and violent they were, and of dread might.

A hundred arms went shooting from the shoulders of each brother,

And from each shoulder fifty heads, ungainly, grew together

And sat upon his sturdy, thickset limbs. They took their stand

Against the Titans in grievous battle, in each massive hand

675 Holding a rocky promontory, a rugged cliff's outcropping.

The Titans meanwhile firmed their ranks zealously; never stopping,

The two sides simultaneously their prowess in war revealed

In equal measure—dreadfully the boundless ocean wailed,

The earth roared hugely and the vaulted sky in answer groaned,

680 Shaken—and high Olympos shook from its base upon the ground

At the onrush of the immortals; and the thundering of their feet,

The din on high of battle rout, unspeakable, the great

Hurtling of their missiles reached the gloomy underworld;

And so those groaning missiles at each other's ranks were hurled,

685 And both sides' shouts and exhortations reached the starry sky,

And so they came together with a massive battle cry.

Now Zeus no longer curbed his strength; at once his breast was filled

With vigor, and all his violence began to be revealed;

And from the sky and from Olympos suddenly he came

690 Ceaselessly hurling thunderbolts and lightning; the flame

Of lightning and the thunder and the thunderbolts flew out

Swiftly from his strong hand, and sacred flame rolled round about;

And everywhere the fertile earth crashed with the shrieking sound

Of burning, the vast forest quaked mightily all around,

695 The ground and the undraining sea and streams of Ocean seethed,

And round the Titans sprung from earth hot blasts of vapor breathed,

And, indescribable, the flame reached the ethereal sky:

A pair of eyes, however strong, would have been blinded by

The flash that from the thunderbolt and blade of lightning gleamed.

700 The infinite space of Chasm held the awful heat; it seemed—

If one could see it with the eye and hear it with the ear—
As if the Heaven had fallen on Earth, colliding with her there,
Such was the massive tumult stirred, the sound of Earth and Sky—
Of her being dashed to ruins and him hurtling from on high,
705   Such was the din of conflict, of the gods in battle clashing.
The winds increased the cloud of dust, the quaking and the crashing;
The thunder, smoky thunderbolt, and lightning flash they bore
(Missiles of mighty Zeus), with all the clamor of the war,
Into the midst of both sides; and the noise of ghastly strife
710   Made known the work of violence and set it in relief.

     The battle turned—until it did, relentlessly together,
Many a combat fierce they fought, each against the other;
But now those at the front lines roused the fighting even more—
Kottos, Briareos, Gyges, who was never tired of war:
715   Out of their sturdy hands three hundred boulders they let fly
In quick succession; these projectiles covered up the sky
Over the Titans' heads; and these they tied in grievous bands
And sent beneath the broad-pathed earth, conquered by their hands,
However overweening in their pride and insolent:
720   As far beneath the earth as earth from sky is they were sent—
For this is how far earth is from the gloomy underworld.
For if from heaven above a brazen anvil had been hurled
And fell nine nights and days, upon the tenth it would come down
To earth; and if that brazen anvil down through the earth were thrown
725   And fell another nine, upon the tenth it would alight
In Tartaros: a brazen wall encases it, and night
Is poured around it at the neck, spread in a triple row:
The roots of earth grow up from it, and those of the sea also.
     The Titan gods beneath the murky gloom are hidden there,
730   According to the counsels of Zeus the Cloud-Gatherer,
In the dank space at the outer edges of monstrous earth.
Poseidon fixed bronze doors on it—they never can go forth—

And driven round the doors upon both sides there runs a wall.
There Gyges, Kottos, and great-hearted Obriareos dwell:
735 The guards of aegis-bearing Zeus, they serve him faithfully.
      The sources and the limits of all things in order lie
There, in that place: the murky earth and the undraining sea,
The hazy, misty underworld itself, the starry sky.
Even the gods abhor it, for it's dank and horrid there,
740 A monstrous, yawning chasm: in the circling of a year,
No man would reach its bottom, if he once had come therein—
Storm after furious storm instead would bear him hither and yon—
And even to the gods it is uncanny, grievous, grim:
Here in this chasm dreary Night obscurely makes her home,
745 And covered up in blackening clouds perpetually it stands.
      Fronting this chasm Atlas holds the broad sky in his hands
And on his head: untiring, he doesn't move; and here,
Conversing with each other, Night and Day meet and draw near,
Exchanging greetings at the door, the great bronze entranceway:
750 When one goes in, the other one goes out—she does not stay;
For never can the two within the house remain together:
Always while one goes round and round about the earth, the other
Remains inside the house until the time has come to go
On her own journey; until then, she's quiet: of these two,
755 One holds the light that sees so much, for mortals who draw breath;
The other one, destructive Night, has Sleep, the brother of Death,
Between her hands, and is concealed amid thick mists and clouds.
      Dark Night's dire children, Sleep and Death, in that place have abodes—
Sleep and Death, two dreaded gods; and never at any times
760 Does Helios behold them with his beams—not when he climbs
Up heavenward in the sky, nor when he goes back down again.
On land and on the broad back of the sea, one of these twain
Is soothing to mankind and dwells in quietness, at rest,
While the other's heart is iron and the spirit in his breast

765 Is pitiless and bronze: on whomsoever he should seize,
766 He takes hold, and is hateful even to the deities.
767   Beyond, the echoing halls of the chthonian god are found,
769 And keeping watch outside them is a dreadful, ruthless hound:
770 With wicked skill he fawns on every victim that appears—
He wags his tail for all of them and perks up both his ears;
But none he lets go out again—he watches at all hours—
And anyone who tries to leave he seizes and devours.
775   There dwells the goddess loathsome to the deathless ones, the dread
Daughter of circling Okeanos, Styx, his eldest bred,
Who far away from the gods within her famous halls resides,
Halls that are vaulted with high stones—and each one of its sides
Has pillars made of silver and is lifted to the sky.
780 Thaumas's daughter, fleet-foot Iris, goes infrequently
On errands there traversing the broad back of the sea;
But when among the deathless ones quarrels and strife arise,
Or if one of the daughters of Olympos should tell lies,
Then Zeus sends Iris out to bring the great oath from afar
785 In a golden ewer—by which the immortals swear,
The legendary, icy water pouring from the height
Of steep rock raised aloft; and far beneath earth's pathways, it
Flows from the sacred stream, a branch of Ocean, through black night.
A tenth part is allotted her, while nine parts are assigned
790 To whirl around the earth and round the broad-backed sea to wind
In silver-swirling eddies tumbling into the salt sea.
Her portion meantime pours off rock—to gods great misery;
For if one of the gods who holds Olympos' snowy peak,
On pouring a libation of that sacred stream, should speak
795 Falsely in oath, he lies, not drawing breath, the whole long year—
He cannot eat ambrosia and to nectar comes not near,
But speechless and unbreathing on a bed, his spirit cowed,
Is covered up in evil coma, as within a shroud.

Moreover, when the year's complete, though this disease is gone,
800 It's followed by a new ordeal, a still more grievous one:
He's banished from the presence of the gods that live forever:
For nine long years he doesn't join their feasts or councils—never;
But in the tenth he goes again and mingles with the gods
In the assembly—those who on Olympos have abodes.
805 Such is the oath the gods set on the eternal water of Styx,
Water that is primordial, and it rushes over the rocks.

    The sources and the limits of all things in order lie
There, in that place: the murky earth and the undraining sea,
The hazy, misty underworld itself, the starry sky.
810 Even the gods abhor it, for it's dank and horrid there;
And there the shining marble gates and brazen threshold are:
With long, unbroken roots it is self-grown, unshakeable.

    On beyond, apart from all the gods, the Titans dwell,
Across the murky Chasm, in the dusky, misty gloom.
815 But Kottos and Gyges at the base of Ocean make their home—
Those allies of loud-thundering Zeus, themselves replete with fame.
Briareos, however, being especially brave, became
Poseidon's kin by marriage, for the Shaker-of-Earth indeed
Gave him Kymopolea, his own daughter, as his bride.

820   But after Zeus had driven out the Titans from the sky,
Prodigious Gaia bore her youngest child, Typhoeus, by
Tartaros—though brought about by golden Aphrodite:
Typhoeus' hands and arms, being made for deeds of strength, were mighty,
And tireless were this strong god's feet; a hundred snaky heads—
825 Those of a dreadful serpent—rose above his shoulder blades,
826 Flickering their murky tongues; and in his awful heads, below
827 The brows, his eyes flashed fire and kept darting to and fro;
829 And each one of the dreadful heads made utterance of its own—
830 Cacophony indescribable, and all in unison!
For while at times their utterance was fit for any god,

At times they bellowed in a mighty bull's voice—loud and proud;
Sometimes they sounded like a lion with a ruthless spirit,
Or else like yelping puppies—it was marvelous to hear it;
835 And when they hissed the echoing sound beneath the hills was heard.
Surely that day, what could not be undone would have occurred,
And he, Typhoeus, would have been the ruler of gods and men,
If not for the keen reckoning of the wise father then:
He thundered a mighty bolt out, and the earth on every side
840 Crashed and echoed fearfully, as did the heavens wide,
The sea, the depths of Tartaros, the running streams of Ocean;
And great Olympos, when he rose, trembled from the motion
Beneath his deathless feet: at this, the earth groaned in reply;
From both of them the heat spread out over the violet sea—
845 From lightning and the fire that from the monster's body came,
As from the flashing storm winds and the thunderbolts aflame;
And everything was fiery hot—sea, sky, the entire earth;
And on the headlands high waves roared on all sides, back and forth,
At the immortals' charge; and there arose an unquenched quaking—
850 Hades, who is the master of the wasted dead, was shaking,
And fear came on the Titans, who with Kronos were deep down
In Tartaros, from the deadly strife and the unending din.
      When Zeus's anger had been raised, he gathered force and took
The lightning flash and thunderbolt that blazed and spewed out smoke,
855 And leaping from Olympos, struck! and everywhere he turned
He caused the awful heads of that dire monster to be burned.
Then when he had subdued him by the strokes that he sent down,
The crippled monster fell—gigantic Gaia gave a groan—
And flame shot from the body of the thunder-stricken lord,
860 Till rugged Aetna's mountain slopes and valleys were devoured
And much of the prodigious earth was burned and wasted in
The preternatural fire's breath—melted, as is tin
When, in the well-aired crucible where craftsmen work their skill,

Heat softens it; or as is iron, strongest thing of all,

865 When subject to a fire burning in hilly vales, at length
It's melted in the sacred earth through great Hephaistos' strength:
So Gaia burned and melted in the blazing fire, and Zeus,
Grieving within his inmost heart, hurled him to Tartaros.
        Out of Typhoeus come damp winds, blasting, boisterous—

870 Except for Notos, Boreas, and clearing Zephyros;
For these, being of divine descent, bring benefits to men,
While randomly the others blow across the sea and then
Inevitably tumble down upon the gloomy ocean,
A bane to humans, breathing up a wicked storm's commotion;

875 And each can blow in diverse ways to scatter and lay low
Ships and sailors: no defense exists against this woe
For humans when encountering these winds upon the sea;
And on the boundless, blooming land all these can equally
Destroy the lovely husbandry, the works of earthborn men,

880 Filling them full of dust through roaring dust storms that cause pain.
        But when the blessèd gods had finished laboring in due course,
They settled the claim to honor of the Titans with brute force,
And then it was they urged farseeing Zeus the Olympian,
On Gaia's cunning counsel, to be sovereign and to reign

885 Over the deathless ones; and he gave each what he was due.
        Now Zeus, as king of gods, took Metis first to wife: she knew
The most and was the wisest of the gods and death-born men.
But when she was about to bear gray-eyed Athena, then
He craftily deceived her with a guileful speech, and down

890 His belly thrust her to the very bowels—this was done
On Gaia's shrewd advice and that of starry Ouranos;
For they two had made known to him that no one else but Zeus
Among the deathless gods should have the kingly privilege;
For otherwise there would have come a crafty lineage

895 From her by fate: the gray-eyed Tritogeneia first, whose force

Was equal to her father's and whose wisdom was not worse;
And next she would have borne a king of gods and men, a child
Having a proud and mighty spirit, passionate, strong-willed;
But Zeus, before that happened, thrust her in his belly, so
900 The goddess might advise him if a thing were good or no.
      He secondly wed Themis, and from her the Horae come,
Eunomia and Dike and Eirene full of bloom—
And they attend upon the works and deeds of mortal men;
The Moirai (Fates), whom Zeus gave greatest honor, bore she then—
905 Clotho and Lachesis and Atropos, who bestow,
On human beings born for death, both happiness and woe.
The lovely child of Okeanos then, Eurynome,
Brought forth the Graces (Charites)—fair-cheeked they are, all three:
Aglaia and Euphrosyne and Thalia also;
910 And from their eyelids, when they looked, desire's stream would flow,
Limb-loosening desire—and how they looked was beautiful.
      Then to Demeter's bed he came, Demeter bountiful:
She bore white-armed Persephone, whom Aidoneus from
Her mother's side did carry off, and Zeus gave her to him;
915 And he made love to lovely-haired Mnemosyne, what is more:
To him the thrice three Muses, golden-filleted, she bore—
Festivity is their delight and pleasure in the song.
Now Leto, having mixed in love with Zeus, before too long
Bore him Apollo and the archer Artemis, a pair
920 Of charming children with whom the other gods cannot compare.
Then last of all he took fresh-blooming Hera for his bride:
She bore him Hebe, Ares, and Eileithuia beside,
When Zeus, the king of gods and men, had lain with her in bed;
And on his own he bore gray-eyed Athena from his head,
925 The feared Atrytone, strife-stirring leader of the host,
The lady whom the uproar of harsh warfare pleases most;
And Hera, without making love, gave birth to glorious

Hephaistos—she was furious and quarreled with her spouse:
Of all the heavenly dwellers, none in skill can equal him.

930   And then from Amphitrite and the loud Earth-Shaker came
Great Triton, mighty far and wide, who occupies the sea:
Beside his lordly father and belovèd mother, he
Dwells in a golden house, a fearsome god. To Ares, who
Can pierce the skin inside a shield, Kytherea bore the two
935 Ferocious gods, Terror and Fear, who drive the ordered ranks
To chaos in the chilling battle—with Ares, he who sacks
Cities; and she bore Harmony, whom Kadmos took as spouse.
    Atlas's daughter Maia bore famed Hermes now to Zeus,
The messenger of the immortals, having climbed his sacred bed.
940 Semele, Kadmos' daughter, bore the radiant boy she'd bred
When she had mixed with Zeus: glad Dionysos, god of wine,
Immortal son of mortal woman—both now are divine.
Alkmene, to be sure, made love with the Cloud-Gatherer,
And forceful Herakles was born in consequence to her.
945 Aglaia to Hephaistos came, the brilliant, limping god,
The youngest of the Graces, in her bloom, to his abode;
And tawny Ariadne, Minos' daughter, came to be
The blooming wife of Dionysos—golden-haired was he;
For him, Zeus made her ageless and undying. When the stout
950 Son of the lovely-limbed Alkmene, Herakles, had put
An end to all his labors, then to Hebe he was wed—
Hebe, the child of mighty Zeus and Hera golden-shod:
This tender girl on snowy Mount Olympos he took to wife.
Because of the great work he did among the gods, his life
955 Is blessed; forever now he dwells, unaging, without pain.
To tireless Helios, Perseis, famed Okeanid, then
Gave birth to Kirke and to King Aietes; he, the son
Of Helios, who brings his light to mortals, shining down,
Married another one of ever-circling Ocean's race—

960 For so the gods ordained: Idyia of the lovely face;

And being subdued by golden Aphrodite's power, Idyia,

In her desire, brought forth the slender-ankled maid, Medea.

Now, farewell, you who dwell upon Olympos, and farewell,

You continents and islands, and beyond, the salt sea-swell;

965 And sing, sweet-sounding Muses of Olympos, daughters of

The aegis bearer, sing of all those goddesses who made love

With mortals—deathless goddesses who lay with death-born men,

And so gave birth to children like the gods.

                                          Demeter then,

One of the heavenly goddesses, bore Ploutos, having known

970 Iasion the hero—in sweet love they lay upon

A thrice-plowed fallow field in fertile Crete. Ploutos goes forth

Over the broad back of the sea and the entire earth;

And he who comes upon the god, into his hands, he gives

Much wealth and many blessings, on account of which he thrives.

975   To Kadmos, Harmony, the child of Aphrodite, bore

Fair-cheeked Agave, Semele, and Ino, what is more,

And Autonoë, whom the long-haired Aristaios wed,

And Polydoros—these, in high-walled Thebes, the goddess bred.

    Kallirhoë, the child of Ocean, mingled in love with mighty

980 Chrysaor, all the while urged on by golden Aphrodite,

And she gave birth to Geryon, who of mortals had most force—

Though Herakles, in sea-swept Erytheia, in due course

Destroyed him—it was on account of the shambling, broad-browed kine.

    Eos bore brazen-armèd Memnon, ruler in the line

985 Of Ethiopians, and, too, the lord Emathion

To Tithonos, and then to Kephalos a shining son,

Powerful Phaithon, a hero like unto the gods; and while

The flower of splendid childhood bloomed resplendent on him still,

The laughter-loving Aphrodite carried him off to where

990 She had her inner sanctum, and she made him overseer,

The spirit-power presiding deep within her sacred shrine.

Aeson's son—according to the immortal gods' design—
Took from King Aietes (whom Zeus fostered) that great king's
Daughter, when the labors that had brought him sufferings—
995   The labors the presumptuous and overbearing one,
King Pelias, in insolence imposed on him—were done;
And when they were accomplished, to Iolkos he took flight,
Bringing on his swift ship the girl whose eyes were shining bright—
Thus Jason did, and took her for his wife in her fresh bloom.
1000 And so, by Jason, shepherd of peoples, being overcome,
She bore a son, Medeos, whom Chiron, Phillyra's son,
Reared up in the mountains; so great Zeus's will was done.

As for the daughters of Nereus, the Old Man of the Sea,
Psamathe, to begin with (a most splendid goddess she),
1005 Bore Phokos to Aiakos—golden Aphrodite's doing;
And Thetis, silver-footed, tamed by Peleus's wooing,
Gave birth to Akhilleus, lionhearted, who breaks men.
And garlanded Kytherea brought forth Aeneas then:
In sweet love with Anchises, the great hero, she had lain
1010 On top of windy Ida, which has many a shaded glen.
And Kirke, child of Helios (he was Hyperion's son),
Through mingling with Odysseus, that stalwart, steadfast one,
Bore Agrios and Latinos, who was blameless and was mighty,
Telegonos as well—all through the work of Aphrodite.
1015 They lived remote on sacred islands, very far away,
And over all the far-renowned Tyrrhenians they held sway.
Kalypso to Odysseus brought forth Nausithoös
When she had made sweet love with him, and bore Nausinoös.

These are the deathless goddesses who lay with mortal men,
1020 And they gave birth to children who were like the gods. Now, then,
Sing, sweet-sounding Muses of Olympos, daughters to
The aegis-bearer, sing about the tribe of women too . . .

WORKS AND DAYS

WORKS AND DAYS

Pierian Muses, be here now—your songs grant mortals fame.
Come, speak about your father Zeus; sing praises to his name.
Glory he sometimes gives to men, and sometimes he gives none:
Some are renowned by his great will; others remain unknown.
5   Easy for him to make men strong, hurl down the strong again,
Humble the prominent in their pride, make the unseen man seen,
Straighten the crooked, blast the arrogant man with a bolt from the sky—
All this does Zeus the high-thunderer, who dwells in his mansion on high.
With justice straighten judgments, lord; in all that you hear and view,
10 Hear me; for, Perses, I would tell only of things that are true.
        Two kinds of Strife upon the earth, not one, have been always.
The first, if she were understood, men would accord her praise.
Blameworthy is the other one (their spirits divide asunder);
Cruel, she fosters wicked war, battle, and heartless plunder.
15 No mortals love this heavy Strife, but by necessity
They give her the honor she is due—to please the gods on high.
As for the other, she was Night's daughter, dark Night's eldest birth.
Kronos's son, high benched in the ether, rooted her deep in the earth.
Better by far she is to men than the other kind:

20 Even the shiftless she stirs to work, who else would give it no mind.
A man who has no work in hand, if he should see another
Rushing to plow and plant his fields and put his house in order,
In envy of his neighbor's wealth will seek prosperity.
This Strife is good for mortal men—you see the reasons why:
25 Potter for dominance contends with potter, joiner with joiner;
Even beggar with beggar vies; singer competes with singer.

Then lay these things up in your heart, and, Perses, neither shirk
Nor let the evil-loving Strife prevent your heart from work
As, listening in the council hall, the wranglings catch your eye.
30 Little concern for wranglings in council hall has he
For whom sufficient sustenance, in season, isn't stored—
Demeter's ripe and golden grain, gathered from old Earth's hoard.
And when you sate yourself in this, then, by all means, advance
Lawsuits to seize what others own—you'll get no second chance;
35 But if you're willing to agree, we can decide the matter
With straight justice, that which comes from Zeus and is far better.
Though we had shared the property, you kept on grabbing things,
To give fat honors and delight to the gift-eating kings.
The verdicts they see fit to bring come with this kind of toll—
40 Fools, they don't know how much more the half is than the whole,
Nor what great good in asphodel and mallow there can be.
The gods hold life—and the means to life—from humanity;
For otherwise in just one day you easily could store
Enough to hold you for a year, although you worked no more.
45 You'd set your oar above the smoke, not to be taken down;
The work of oxen, patient mules would soon be done and gone.

But Zeus, being angered in his heart, hid it away from us,
Having been crookedly deceived by sly Prometheus.
He, on account of this, devised for humans pain and dole,
50 Concealed the fire, which the noble son of Iapetos stole
In a hollow stalk of fennel back for mankind's use,

Unheeded by the wise counselor, thunder-delighting Zeus.

    Then the Cloud-Gatherer in rage addressed the Titan thus:

"Your schemes surpass all other schemes, son of Iapetos;

55 Now you rejoice at having stolen fire, outwitting me:

Much misery both for yourself, yourself and men to be.

To them in recompense for fire, I shall bequeath a woe,

Which they will cherish in their hearts, although it lays them low."

    So spoke the father of gods and men, and laughed out loud; then bade

60 Hephaistos, the famed artisan, at once to mix and knead

Water and earth, and put in strength and speech distinctly human,

Make it in aspect like a deathless goddess, but a woman,

A lovely maiden and in her form desirable to men;

And bade Athena teach her how to ply the loom; and then

65 Bade golden Aphrodite pour grace on her shining hair,

And painful longing and regret and limb-devouring care;

Last, to put in a currish mind and thievish character,

Commanded Hermes, slayer of dogs, Hermes the messenger.

    So spoke his lordship, Kronion Zeus—they did as they were told.

70 And from the earth forthwith the famous Dextrous One did mold

The likeness of a modest maid by Kronos' son's design;

The gray-eyed goddess did adorn and dress her; the divine

Graces and revered Persuasion placed upon her skin

Golden chains and necklaces; the fair-haired Hours did twine

75 Garlands of flowers about her head, the freshest they could gather;

And Pallas Athena on her skin fit all these things together.

Then in her breast the slayer of dogs, Hermes the messenger,

Fashioned lies and wheedling words and a thievish character;

And the gods' herald gave her a voice, by the thunderer's design,

80 And called this woman the All-Gifted one, Pandora, because the divine

Olympians all gave her a gift and as a gift did give

Her as a woe to mortal men, who must earn their bread to live.

    The father, when he had conceived this steep, resistless snare,

To Epimetheus with the gift he sent the messenger;

85 And Epimetheus did not consider what his brother

Prometheus had warned concerning gifts from Zeus, that rather

Than keep what the Olympian gave, send them all back again,

Lest somehow they turn out to be a woe to mortal men:

Holding the woe he had received, he knew it—only then.

90   For previously the tribes of men lived happily on earth,

91 Remote from suffering, from painful labor, and from dearth,

92 And all the baleful maladies that bring life to an end—

94 Before the woman lifted off the jar's lid with her hand

95 And scattered out its contents, bringing humans grievous pain:

And only hope in its unbroken dwelling did remain

Inside the jar beneath its rim—away it never flew:

She thrust the lid back on the jar before that could ensue,

As Zeus the aegis-bearing god, gatherer of clouds, designed;

100 But troubles that are numberless wander among mankind.

The earth and sea are full of ills, of things to be abhorred;

Diseases come by day and night and of their own accord;

Continually they come to men in silence, bearing woe,

For Zeus the cunning took away their voices long ago;

105 So all attempts to flee the mind of Zeus are bound to fail.

But if you're willing I shall tell the gist of another tale:

How, from a single origin, mortals and gods are sprung.

Now, store it up within your heart—with skill it shall be sung.

The deathless ones, who dwell upon Olympos, as of old,

110 In the beginning made a race of mortals that was gold.

These people lived in Kronos' time, when he was heaven's king;

Like gods they lived, with carefree heart, remote from suffering.

No toil or misery was theirs; to them there never came

Wretched old age—in feet and hands they always were the same,

115 Rejoicing in the feast the while, apart from every woe,

And when they died it was as if mild sleep had laid them low.

They were endowed with all things good; spontaneously then
The earth bore rich, abundant fruit; and these contented men,
Living in peace, enjoyed its works and all its many goods,
120 Abundantly supplied with sheep, beloved of the blessèd gods.

Now, since the time this happy race was covered up by earth,
As tutelary deities Zeus bids them still go forth
To serve as guardians of men, and at his high behest
Watch over suits and wicked deeds, clothed in a shroud of mist.
125 Givers of wealth, they roam the world, beneficent and kind—
This is the kingly privilege that they have been assigned.

They who upon Olympos have their dwellings fashioned then
A second, much inferior race, a silver race of men,
Neither in understanding nor in stature like the other.
130 A hundred years the child remained, coddled by its mother,
A baby in the house, but big! frolicking all that time;
And when at last they were full grown and come into their prime,
They only lived a few short years—in suffering and pain:
Fools, from reckless violence they never could refrain,
135 And would not serve the deathless ones—it went against their pride—
Nor at the holy altars of the blessed would they preside
As custom has decreed to men; so Zeus the Kronion
Hid them away in rage at what these men had left undone,
The honors that they did not give the Olympian deities.
140 The earth has covered them as well, this second race, but these
Beneath its confines now are called the mortal-blessed-below;
For honor still accompanies these second ones, them too.

Then Zeus the father made another race of mortal ones,
In nothing similar to the silver—this third race he made bronze
145 And of the ash tree—mighty, dire, and in their arrogance
Given to Ares' groaning deeds and acts of violence.
They ate no bread—so dauntless and so adamant their spirit,
So huge, resistless was their strength, that nothing could come near it;

And irresistible the arms that from their shoulders grew
150 Upon their brawny bodies; bronze their arms and houses too
And implements: they worked in bronze—dark iron there was none.
By one another's arms they were subdued and overthrown,
And nameless to chill Hades' moldy dwelling they went down;
For howsoever terrible and mighty they were grown,
155 Black death took them—they resigned the bright light of the sun.
When they were covered in their turn, when this race too was gone,
Zeus on the ever-nourishing earth made yet another one;
And these the son of Kronos made more righteous, better far,
A race of heroes, godlike men—men of this fourth race are
160 Called demigods; they came before us on the unbounded earth,
And were destroyed by dreadful war. Some who had ventured forth
To fight in battle for the flocks of Oedipus were slain
Beneath the seven gates of Thebes, in the Kadmean domain;
And some whom ships conveyed across the great gulf of the sea
165 To Troy, were swallowed up by death in its finality,
166 All for the sake of Helen, for her of the lovely hair.
167 To others, life and livelihood and homes where no men are
168 Were given by Zeus the father in the earth's remotest part:
170 Here were these heroes settled—they dwell with carefree heart
Beside deep-eddying Ocean, in the Islands of the Blessed.
Three times a year the fertile earth grows ripe and is increased,
And happy are the heroes whom it bears delightful grain.
I wish that I were not among this last, fifth race of men,
175 But either dead already or had afterwards been born;
For this race now is iron indeed, and never, night or morn,
Will leave off from their suffering, worn down by toil and woe.
The gods will give them harsh and grievous cares, but even so,
They too shall have a share of good, mixed though it be with pain—
180 Also, Zeus will eradicate this race of mortal men:
In such a time when at their birth babies turn out to be

Gray at the temples; when fathers and sons have lost all harmony;
When the relation of comrade to comrade fails, and of host to guest;
When brother no longer is friend to brother, as formerly in the past.
185 They'll treat their parents with disdain as soon as they are old,
Heartlessly finding fault with them in accents harsh and cold;
And ignorant of the punishment the gods mete, as they are,
They'll not be likely to repay their parents for their care.
Taking the law into their hands, they'll pillage and destroy
190 Each other's cities; gratitude shall no man then enjoy
Who righteously serves justice and who keeps his oath, but him
Who's wicked and does violence—that man they will esteem.
Might shall make right: the evil man his better will subdue
By speaking crooked words and swearing oaths upon them too;
195 And shrieking Envy that delights in harming wretched men,
With foul-mouthed, hate-filled face shall be each man's companion then.
Forsaking humankind to be among the deathless gods,
Leaving the earth's broad pathways for the Olympian abodes,
Their lovely bodies mantled in white cloaks without a stain,
200 Restraint and Censure will depart—sad sufferings remain
For death-born men, and no defense from evil will avail.
But now—though they themselves will know—I'll tell the kings a tale.
Unto a dapple-necked nightingale a hawk had this to say,
As, gripping her fast in his curved claws, he bore her far away
205 High in the clouds; she, piteously, pierced through and through, did grieve;
But he—in an imperious tone—addressed this narrative:
"Why are you screaming, lunatic? You're caught by one much stronger;
And where I take you, you shall go, although you be a singer.
I'll make a dinner of you or release you, as I choose:
210 To set oneself in folly against superiors is to lose
Victory and to incur shame amid sufferings."
So spoke the swiftly flying hawk, bird with the wide-spread wings.
Perses, pay heed to righteousness; don't add to violence:

It is an evil for the man of little consequence;

215 Nor can the splendid man with ease endure that heavy load
When he confronts calamities; much better does the road—
The other one—to righteousness fulfill you in the end;
But, till he suffers, this the fool will never comprehend.
For Oath is swift to run alongside judgments that are bent,

220 And Justice, when she's dragged about, clamors for punishment;
And though gift-eating, crooked judges lead her up and down,
She doubles back upon the haunts and habits of the town
In tears; and in a shroud of mist, with evil lies in wait
For those who drive her out by not distributing her straight.

225 But those who give to strangers and to natives what is due,
Who keep the paths of justice straight, whatever may ensue,
For them the city flourishes—its people thrive therefore;
Peace that nurtures children reigns throughout the land, and war
With all its woes is not ordained by Zeus who sees afar.

230 Nor ever with straight-judging men is Famine present, nor
Disaster, but they feast upon the fruits of what they till.
Earth bears them a rich livelihood: the oak upon the hill
Bears acorns in its branches, in its trunk bears honey bees,
And wooly sheep are laden with the weight of heavy fleece,

235 And women bring forth children who are like their fathers; so,
Continually prospering, on ships they do not go—
Because of the abundant fruit the fertile grain-lands bear.

To those who practice violence, make wicked deeds their care,
Just retribution is assigned by Zeus who sees afar.

240 Often a single evil man, reckless finagler,
Makes an entire city suffer through his iniquities;
From heaven the son of Kronos sends great woe to such as these:
Famine and plague together, so that people get sick and die,
Babies no longer are born to women, households diminish—by

245 The shrewdness of Olympian Zeus, who also yet again

May choose to destroy the citadel or the army of such men,
Or vengeance the son of Kronos may wreak on their ships upon the sea.
    Kings, you had better yourselves observe this justice carefully;
For near among men there are deathless ones, yes, deathless ones nearby,
250   And they watch such men as with crooked judgments, judgments that
        cheat and lie,
Grind others down without paying heed to the gods' harsh punishment.
Thrice countless are the immortals who as guardians are sent
Upon the ever-nourishing earth by Zeus the Kronion
To watch over suits and wicked deeds shrouded in mist; unknown,
255   They roam the world continually, traveling up and down.
    But Justice is a maiden and the daughter of Zeus, and she
Is splendid and revered among the Olympian company;
So if someone should do her harm or heap her with abuse
Through crooked talk, she goes forthwith to sit with Father Zeus,
260   And speaks about men's unjust mind, their ruinous intent—
Until the entire people pays for judgments that are bent
By those who speak perversely and the recklessness of kings.
Straighten your utterances, my lords; be wary of these things—
Gift-eaters that you are, forget all judgments that are deformed;
265   For he who harms another is himself by others harmed,
And wicked schemes most heavily upon the schemer fall.
The eye of Zeus, seeing everything and understanding all,
Even, if it should choose, beholds these things; nor does it fail
To mark the kind of justice that the city holds within.
270   As things now stand I couldn't wish that I or a son of mine
Should act with righteousness toward men; for it would be his bane—
If the unrighteous had more rights—to be a righteous man;
But this, I think, the wise counselor is not about to impart.
    Perses, do understand these things and store them in your heart:
275   Attentively heed Justice and forget all violence;
For Zeus the son of Kronos has laid down this ordinance,

That whereas fish and wingèd birds and wild beasts of all sorts
May eat each other, righteousness being absent from their hearts,
To mankind he gave righteousness, and that by far is best.
280 For if a man by habit speaks the things he knows are just,
Farseeing Zeus the thunderer grants him prosperity;
But he who willingly, when bearing witness, tells a lie,
Injuring Justice by that act, is harmed beyond all cure:
In later times his offspring will be rendered more obscure,
285 While those of one who faithfully has kept his oath do well.

      Perses, it's for your profit that I say this, you great fool;
For Badness in abundance can be had, as you're aware:
The path that leads to her is smooth; her dwelling-place is near—
The deathless ones placed sweat and toil before Prosperity,
290 And rugged at the start and steep and long the path will be
That leads to her; but when at last the summit comes in view,
In fact, although the climb was hard, it's easy now to do.

      That man is best who all things by himself can apprehend,
And pondering where the future lies, can profit in the end;
295 And he is good as well who trusts to speakers that are wise;
But one who neither thinks himself nor hearing good advice
Lodges it up within his heart, that man is worst in kind.
But you, who always keep our remonstrations well in mind,
You, Perses, of divine descent, must work so Hunger will
300 Despise you, and the lovely-wreathed, revered Demeter fill
Your granary with livelihood; for Hunger, as you see,
Is the companion of the workless man—his misery.
Both gods and mortals disapprove of all such workless ones,
And such as in their character resemble stingless drones,
305 Who, workless, eat and wear away the labor of the bees.
306 Embrace due order in your works, so that your granaries
307 May be replete with sustenance, a plethora in season.
308 If men are rich in sheep and have much wealth, it's for this reason;

309 For dearer to the deathless ones by far is he who works—
311 There is no blame for him who works, only for him who shirks;
312 And if you work the workless man shortly will envy you
313 As you gain wealth; success and fame to wealthy men accrue;
314 Regardless of your circumstances, work is what's best to do.
315 If only from what others own you'd turn your witless mind
And, taking thought for your livelihood, work! as I have enjoined.
Restraint makes no provision that can profit men in need;
Restraint, from which great hurts as well as helps likewise proceed,
Is near to poverty as boldness is to plenty.
                                                    Goods
320 Are not meant to be seized by men but given by the gods;
For if someone gains riches for himself by means of force,
Or seizes booty with false words, as often in the course
Of human life occurs, just then, when Shame is driven out
By Shamelessness, and gain besots the mind of every lout,
325 Then do the gods obscure that man and shrink his household too:
Prosperity with him but for a little while will go.
    To one who harms a suppliant or stranger, this applies,
Also to one who climbs on his own brother's bed and lies
In secret with his brother's wife against all decency;
330 To one who injures orphans out of sheer stupidity,
And one who hurls abuse against his aged progenitor,
Assailing him with bitter words when he is at death's door:
With such a one is Zeus himself enraged, and in the end
A harsh requital for his unjust acts will surely send.
335 But altogether keep your witless mind from things like these,
And make such offerings as you can to the deathless deities:
Upon the altars—purely, cleanly—burn the splendid thighs.
At other times, with incense and libations sacrifice,
Both when sacred daylight comes and when you take your rest,
340 So that the holy ones may hold you gracious in their breast

And you can buy another's land, not have him buy your own.

      Invite your friend to dinner; leave your enemy alone;

And him especially invite, the one who lives nearby;

For if misfortune should befall you on your property,

345   Neighbors will come just as they are, but kinsmen must get dressed.

An evil neighbor is a bane; with good ones you are blessed;

A share in a good neighbor is a prize, a precious boon:

No oxen would be lost if evil neighbors were unknown.

Receive fair measure from your neighbor; give it back again

350   In like measure, and even more amply, if you can,

So that there's someone you can trust when next you have occasion.

      Avoid ill-gotten gain—ill-gotten gain spells devastation;

Befriend a friend and call for help from one who calls on you;

Give to the man who's wont to give, not one who tells you, "No!"

355   A giver gives to those who give, not to the niggardly:

Giving is good but Seizing bad—a giver of death is she;

For if one freely gives a gift, even a thing not slight,

The very act will bring him joy—his heart will take delight;

But should a man, because he trusts in shamelessness, just seize,

360   Though it be but a little thing, he makes his spirit freeze;

For if you add a little to a little frequently,

It quickly turns to something big—it grows, as you can see,

And he who adds to what is there makes hunger burn the less.

It's not what's stored up in the house that gives a man distress;

365   For out of doors is out of reach—what's in the house is better;

And while it's excellent to take from what's on hand, it's bitter

Anguish in the breast to need, to lack what isn't there.

      Ponder this wisdom. Take your fill of a full or empty jar;

Be sparing when it's half-way full: thrift at the lees is vain.

370   Secure the wages you have pledged a friend or any man,

And with your brother, laugh, but get a witness, even so;

For trust can do men damage, much as lack of trust can do;

Nor let a woman's rounded ass deceive you in your mind—
She'll empty out your granary with wheedling words, you'll find;
375   For trusting in a woman is like trusting robbers. May
A single son be born to keep his father's house: that way,
Wealth will increase within the halls; and may you, an old man,
Die with the thought you leave behind another, your own son.

      Yet Zeus could easily provide for plenitude untold;
380   More care for work by more would bring increases manifold;
So if the spirit in your breast longs for prosperity,
Then do as I have said and work—yes, work unceasingly.

      When the Pleiades have risen, just before the sun,
Begin to reap; begin to plant before they set at dawn.
385   Those daughters of Atlas are obscured and never can be found
For forty nights and days until the year again turns round;
But when the harvest blade is honed, they twinkle in the sky.
This law is of the land—for those who dwell hard by the sea,
And those who in the hollow glens that skirt the mountainside,
390   Far from the swelling sea, in fertile pasturelands abide.
Then, naked, sow and, naked, plow (I say it for a reason),
And, naked, reap the corn, if you desire in good season
To put Demeter's works in order, each crop, as is proper,
Growing in its own due time, so you won't be a pauper
395   Crouching in the homes of others, doing no earthly good,
As now you come to me once more. I hope it's understood,
I'll measure nothing further out—Perses, no more for you!
Go work, you fool! It's what the gods have set mankind to do;
Or one day, with your wife and children, sick at heart indeed,
400   You'll have to beg for your livelihood from neighbors that pay no heed.
It may be that you'll get results two times or even three,
But if you vex them further you'll be talking fruitlessly.
Nothing can be accomplished with fine words; you'd better ponder
How to release yourself from debt and free yourself from hunger.

405   A household first, a woman, and an ox is what you need—
A female slave, unmarried, who can plow and sow the seed.
You must yourself make ready all your goods and household gear:
Don't ask another—he'll say no and leave you standing there
In want, the season passing and your yield becoming less.
410 Don't leave things till tomorrow out of utter laziness!
The man whose work is fruitless, who postpones, has never filled
His barn; it takes attention to how crops increase their yield,
And work-postponing men are always wrestling with blight.
     When the heat of the piercing sun diminishes in might,
415 And autumn emanates from Zeus, who brings down cooling rain,
And afterwards when humans feel much lighter in their skin—
For then the dog star Sirius only brief time will loom
Over the heads of human beings, born as they are to doom,
Daily, and of its share of night increasingly partakes.
420 The tree you cut with iron isn't wormy then; it shakes
And scatters leaves upon the ground, letting no new shoots bud.
Then recollect the season's task: to fell and chop the wood.
     Cut your mortar three feet wide, your pestle three cubits long;
And cut your axle seven feet—that way you won't go wrong;
425 Or if you make it one foot more, you can hew yourself off a maul.
For a cart that stands ten palms in length, carve out a three-span wheel.
Many bent logs can be found: bring it home, whenever you find one
    that yields
Its trunk for a plow-tree, made of holm oak; search over mountains
    and fields.
That will be strongest for plowing with oxen, as soon as the carpenter,
430 Athena's slave, bolting it firmly, fixes it to the share
And fastens it to the pole with dowels. Don't spare yourself the pain
Of keeping two plows for yourself at home in your domain:
One nature-made, one made by man—you'll see it's worth the bother;
For if you break one, you can yoke your oxen to the other.

435 The clearest, strongest poles are of sweet bay or elm; the share
Should be of oak, the tree, holm oak. Go get yourself a pair
Of nine-year-old male oxen, for their strength is at its height:
They've reached their prime but still have youth; they work and do
    not fight;
Nor do they quarrel in the furrow, shattering the plow,
440 Leaving the work unfinished and with nothing you can do.
Have a man of forty follow these, who's strong and, having fed
Upon a double portion of an eight-pieced loaf of bread,
Is careful at his task and drives a furrow straight, no longer
Peering around for friends his age, but bent on work. No younger
445 Man is ever better than a man like this at throwing
Seeds in such a way as to avoid all over-sowing;
For younger men are keen upon their comrades.

                                Every year,
When first you hear the crane's voice, be attentive, be aware,
And as on high amid the clouds she screeches, make your plans:
450 She signifies the plowing time and indicates the rains
Of winter, and she bites into the heart of oxless men:
Then feed the curved-horned cattle that you keep inside your pen.
"Give me a cart and oxen" is an easy thing to say—
And easily rejected: "They have work enough today."
455 A man may dream he's wealthy, so he'll build a cart, he thinks:
The fool has never reckoned that it takes a hundred planks!
Make it your care beforehand to arrange these things at home.

        Soon as the plowing time makes known to mortals it is come,
You and your slaves alike should rush into it eagerly;
460 In the season right for plowing, when the ground is wet or dry,
Hurry to till it early, so your field is full of grain;
Retill it early in season and it will not be in vain;
And sow the land that's fallow while the soil is dry and loose:
What's fallow wards off ruin and soothes Hades.

465 Chthonian and Demeter, goddess undefiled and pure,
That her sacred grain may grow until it's heavy and mature,
When you start in plowing, as you grip the top of the pole
And with a switch come down upon the oxen as they pull
The yoke-peg with the strapping. Let a slave who has a hoe,

470 Following close behind you, hide the scattered seed you sow,
So as to make the birds work; for humans that die need order:
Disorder's worst for mortal men and makes their lives much harder.
This way the thick-grown ears of corn down to the ground will bend,
If the Olympian should grant abundance in the end,

475 And you can sweep the cobwebs from the storage bins and jars,
Rejoicing in the livelihood you take from what's indoors,
Well stocked until you reach bright spring, not casting, in your need,
Glances on others—other men will look to you for aid.
        But if you plow the noble earth when the sun has turned again,

480 You'll reap sitting and only clasp a little bit of grain,
Covered in dust as you bind the sheaves, a cheerless man, and you
Will carry it off in a basket, the admiration of few.
The mind of aegis-bearing Zeus this way or that may tend
At different times—too difficult for men to comprehend;

485 For even if you plow too late, there is this remedy:
When first the cuckoo cuckoos in the leaves of the oak tree,
Giving delight to mortals on the boundless earth, just then,
For three days straight, incessantly, Zeus may bring down rain
Rising to an ox's hoof—not higher or less high:

490 This way the later-plowing man might with the early vie.
Then store this up within your heart, and keep it safely there:
Let neither spring nor coming autumn rain escape your care.
        Pass by the smith's bench and the warmth of the lounging hall or den
In the wintry season when the icy cold keeps men

495 From working (the determined man can much improve his home),

Lest during wretched winter Want and Hardship overcome
You, and you squeeze with shriveled hand a swollen foot.
The workless man, subsisting on hope's hollowness, without
A livelihood, will conjure many evil things indeed:
500 For Hope makes no provision that can profit men in need,
And he who lounges in the hall has no sure livelihood.
So, say unto your slaves while yet the summer still holds good:
"Build yourselves huts, for summer days will not be here always."
    Avoid the coming evil days, the oxen-flaying days
505 Of January and the frosts that cruel then are grown
Upon the ground when Boreas his bitter breath has blown.
He breathes through horse-nurturing Thrace and onto the wide sea,
Stirring it up, with land and forest roaring furiously;
And towering oaks and massive fir trees in the mountain glen
510 He brings down to the earth that feeds all living beings when
He falls upon them; then the vast forest howls and wails:
The beasts, shivering, put their tails beneath their genitals;
Even the ones covered with fur, Boreas, you see,
Blows through with his bitter breath, thick-coated though they be;
515 And even through the hide of an ox—that doesn't stop him, no;
And even through the long-haired goat he blows—but does not blow
Through flocks of sheep because their fleece is full; though here he fail,
His breath upon the agèd man will blow him like a wheel.
Not through the maiden's tender skin does Boreas blow, for she
520 Remains with her dear mother in the house continually,
With golden Aphrodite's works as yet being unacquainted;
And when she's bathed her soft, young skin and amply anointed
Herself with oil, then she lies down deep in the inner house
Upon a winter's day—the time the boneless octopus
525 Gnaws his foot in the fireless, dank haunt that is his station;
For not to him does Helios point out a habitation
Where he can feed, but in the lands of dark-skinned men he roams,

Shining more tardily in those the Hellenes have their homes.
Lastly the forest dwellers, horned and hornless ones, will then
530　Wretchedly grind their teeth as they take flight through copse and glen.
This is the feeling in each heart, the overweening care
Of those who seek in hollow rocks a covert or close-packed lair.
Then are they like the three-legged man whose curved back bends around—
His head habitually is turned; he gazes on the ground;
535　Like him they wander here and there, avoiding the white snow.
　　　Then clothe yourself when that time comes the way I tell you to:
Wear a soft cloak with a long-hemmed tunic against your skin
(Weave many threads of woof into a warp that's scant and thin),
And wrap the cloak around yourself so that your hair lies still
540　And doesn't stand erect upon your body when days grow chill.
Tie fitted sandals round your feet, lined thick with felt inside,
Fashioned from the hide of an ox you've killed, not one that died;
And from your firstborn kids stitch skins with cattle gut together
To make a cape to shield your back from rain and icy weather.
545　Do this when the frost first comes; and have a well-made hat
Of felt upon your head to keep your ears from getting wet.
Daybreak is always icy cold when Boreas descends,
And from the starry skies to earth at dawn a mist extends
Over the fields of prosperous men (it makes the young wheat grow);
550　And drawing moisture out of rivers that forever flow,
It's lifted high aloft on blustery gales above the land:
Sometimes it falls at evening with the rain or with the wind
When Thracian Boreas drives the clouds in thick confusion forth:
Before this happens, finish work and head home to your hearth,
555　Lest some dark storm-cloud from the skies chance to envelop you
Completely, till your skin is soaked, your clothing drenched all through.
This is the very cruelest month, so guard against it well—
The height of wintertime, for beasts and human beings cruel.
　　　You ought to give your oxen half their rations and allow

560 Your man a little more than half—the nights are longer now
     And thus a help. Heed all these things through the closing of the year,
     And balance out the nights and days together till once more
     The mother of all things, the Earth, brings back her varied produce.
         When sixty days of winter are accomplished by Lord Zeus,
565 After the turning of the year, the star Arcturus then
     Forsakes the holy stream of Okeanos once again,
     And newly is arisen at the twilight in a blaze;
     And after him the daughter of Pandion sings her lays,
     The early-wailing swallow, and she moves into men's sight:
570 Then prune your vines before she brings in spring, for this is right.
         When he-who-carries-his-own-house climbs up the vines you've grown,
     To flee the Pleiades, the time for hoeing's done and gone;
     So hone your scythes and stop your household slaves from slumbering on.
     Avoid the shady benches and the sleeping until dawn
575 In the harvest season when the sun dries up the skin:
     That's when you hurry homeward and you bring the harvest in,
     Getting up at daybreak so your property can grow.
         Morning takes up a third of all your work; and as you know,
     Morning will bear you forward on the road that you must go,
580 And in your labor; morning, having once appeared, will show
     Many men on journeys, many oxen yoked also.
         When the artichoke's in bloom and the cicada in the tree,
     The musical cicada, spreads continual melody,
     Sweet-toned from beneath its wings in the wearying summer sea-
585 son, then the goats are fattest and the wine is at its best,
     The women are most wanton and the men are most depressed.
     When Sirius the dog star dries the head up and the knee,
     And skin is parched beneath the burning sun, then let there be
     Some shade beneath a rock and wine from Biblos and the bread
590 That's made from milk and milk from goats—the last the kids are fed
     Before they're weaned—and meat from newborn kids and leaf-fed kine

That haven't given birth; and then you drink the sparkling wine,
Sitting in the shade and filled with food, your heart at ease,
Faced in the direction of a strong Zephyrean breeze;
595 And from an ever-flowing stream—unmuddied, clear, and clean—
Pour three parts water with a fourth of wine that's blended in.

At such time as Orion in his mighty strength appears,
Exhort your slaves to thresh the sacred grain Demeter bears,
In an open, well-aired space, on a rounded threshing floor.
600 Then measure into ordered bins the grain you need to store,
So that you have your livelihood laid in at home; and then
Bestir yourself and a hired man who's homeless to obtain
A girl who's childless—one who's busy nursing is no good.
And take care of your sharp-toothed dog: don't stint upon his food,
605 Lest one who sleeps by day and prowls by night should carry off
Your property; and cart in hay and chaff till there's enough
To feed and bed the oxen, mules, and asses. Finally,
Allow your slaves to cool their knees, your oxen to roam free.

When Sirius and Orion reach the midpoint in the sky,
610 And the rosy-fingered Dawn can see Arcturus rising high,
Then, Perses, pluck the clusters of the grape and bring them home.
Expose them to the sun until ten days have come and gone;
Then shade them for another five, and on the sixth day pour
The gift of much-rejoicing Dionysos in a jar.
615 When the Pleiades and Hyades, Orion in his might,
Are setting, then remember that the season now is right
For plowing: may the seed you sow lie firm beneath the earth.
And though desire for sailing stormy seas should draw you forth,
At such time as the Pleiades are hurtling in flight
620 Toward the misty sea, before Orion in his might,
And gales of every kind of wind are raging furiously,
No longer should you sail your ships upon the wine-dark sea,
But keep on working, mindful of the earth, as I command.

Prop up your ship with rocks when you have hauled it onto land,
625 So as to curb the muscle of the water-blasting winds;
And pull the plug of the bilge-drain so the thunderstorms Zeus sends
Won't rot the timbers. When you've trimmed and stowed away the sail,
Then store your gear within your house securely without fail,
And hang your well-made steering oar above the smoke, and then
630 Remain on land until the time for sailing comes again.

At that time, haul your ship to sea, and ready its freight within,
So you can bring home for yourself the profit that you win,
Just as our father, foolish Perses, yours and mine, thought good:
He sailed on shipboard on the seas to gain a livelihood,
635 And one day came here, having crossed the broad, abundant sea,
And in his black ship left behind Aeolian Cumae. He
Was fleeing not from plenty, from wealth or prosperity,
But evil want, what Zeus bestows on men—from poverty.
In Askra, a town near Helicon, a poor one, he abode—
640 Vile in the winter, grievous in summer, not ever any good.

Perses, all tasks are seasonal—this you should keep in mind—
And those concerning seamanship especially, you'll find.
Bestow your praise on a little boat, but stow your freight in one
Bigger—the bigger the cargo, the bigger the profit won—
645 Provided the fair winds don't change to wicked gales instead.

So when it happens that you turn your witless thoughts to trade,
Yearning to flee from debt and mirthless hunger's misery,
Then I will demonstrate the rules of the loud-roaring sea—
Though no wise skilled in sailing or in ships or shipcraft skilled;
650 For never yet on shipboard on the broad sea have I sailed,
Save to Euboea across from Aulis—by way of which the host
Of the Achaians through the winter gathered before they crossed
From sacred Greece to Ilium, where lovely women dwell.
There to the games for warlike Amphidamus did I sail
655 To Chalcis (many were the games for that great-hearted one

His sons had caused to be proclaimed); and there I say I won
And carried off the double-handled tripod for my song,
And set it for the Muses as a prize on Helicon,
The place where I first mounted up to sweet-toned melody.
660 And this is what I know of bolted ships that sail the sea;
But all the same I'll tell you of the aegis-bearer's will,
For the Muses, teaching me to sing, gave me unbounded skill.

       After the summer solstice, at the end of fifty days,
Just when the season of fatigue enters its final phase,
665 That is the time for mortals to set sail: you will not then
Shatter your ship, and neither will the sea lay waste your men—
Unless the one who shakes the earth, Poseidon, should be bent
On killing them, or Zeus himself should harbor this intent;
For through them all things come to pass, all things both good and ill.
670 The winds are steady at that time, the sea is favorable:
So, trusting in the winds, haul out your swift ship to the sea
And lay your freight on board without the least anxiety;
But hurry to come back again as quickly as you can,
And don't wait till the new wine comes or for the autumn rain,
675 Or till the winter's on its way or for the fierce South Wind
Stirring the sea together with the storms that Zeus may send
In autumn or late summer, which can make seafaring hard.

       Springtime is the other time when sailing is preferred,
Just when the leaf of the fig tree at the very tip of the bough
680 Seems to men as wide as the footprint made on earth by the crow:
The sea is fit for sailing then, for ships to venture out;
And this is springtime sailing—though for my part I do not
Praise it, for it doesn't please my spirit but is to me
A risk men seize, an evil they escape with difficulty.
685 Yet these are things that ignorance compels mankind to do;
For property is life to wretched mortals, as you know.
Dying amidst the waves is something terrible indeed;

So mull these matters over in your heart, as I have said.

  Don't load your hollow ships with all the earthly goods you own,
690 But keep a larger portion back and ship a smaller one;
For coming to grief is terrible amidst the swelling sea,
And dreadful if, by loading down your cart excessively,
You break the axle, ruining the wares you wished to trade:
Everything has its proper season; limits must be obeyed.

695 Take a wife into your dwelling at such time as you
Have reached the age of thirty years, give or take a few:
That is the proper time for getting married, as I've said.
The woman should ripen for four years, and in the fifth should wed.
Marry a young girl you can shape and teach good character;
700 In preference to all others, one you've known and who lives near.
Don't marry for the mirth of all your neighbors, if you can;
For while there's nothing better than a good wife for a man,
There's nothing worse than one who's bad—a glutton who will snatch!
And though her husband's vigilant, burns him without a match,
705 And, as she does, delivers him to premature old age.

  Be mindful of the deathless ones; take heed against their rage.
Don't treat your friend as if he were your brother, but if you do,
Be careful not to work him harm—a quarrel will ensue.
Don't lie for the sake of lying, but if he has once begun,
710 Either with a nasty word or hateful action done,
Be sure to pay him back in kind; but if he should again
Regard you as his friend and recompense you for your pain,
Accept him; for the man who changes friendships constantly
Is worthless—let no untoward thoughts your outward looks belie.

715 Neither be called too friendly nor unfriendly to a guest,
A crony of the worst of men nor troubler of the best;
And never dare reproach a man for crushing poverty—
It breaks the heart but is bestowed by the gods who never die;
For sparingness of speech is best: the tongue, a precious treasure,

720　Confers the greatest grace on men when it runs in good measure;

　　And slander swiftly lighting on the slanderer is increased.

　　Don't be a boor when many guests have gathered for a feast;

　　For when the expense is shared, the pleasure's most, the cost is least.

　　And never pour the sparkling wine with unwashed hands at dawn

725　To Zeus the son of Kronos or another deathless one;

　　For then the gods won't hear your prayers—they'll spit them out with hate!

　　Don't turn to face into the sun when you stop to urinate;

　　And even when the sun's gone down or hasn't risen yet,

　　Don't do it in the roads or, as you're walking, off the roads,

730　Or naked; for the nights belong unto the blessèd gods.

　　The one who does it squatting is a wise and godly man,

　　Or else he does it at the wall of a courtyard, if he can.

　　Don't let your genitals, when smeared with semen, be in view

　　When you are near the hearth—for that's a thing you must not do.

735　And don't beget your family after a funeral feast,

736　But after one for the deathless gods—the omens then are best.

757　Into the mouths of streams that flow to sea you may not void,

758　Nor yet at fountains—these are things you always should avoid;

759　And do not move your bowels in them—this also is denied.

737　Don't ever wade across the flow of rivers that are gleaming

738　Before you've prayed and looked into the beauty of their streaming,

739　In glorious clear water having first performed ablution;

740　For he who'd cross a river with his hands mired in pollution,

　　The gods resent him and they give him pains in years to come.

　　Don't cut the dry nail from the new, from fingers or from thumb,

　　With the gleaming iron at the gods' rich festival.

　　Don't ever put the ladle on the top of the mixing bowl

745　When people still are drinking, lest an awful fate ensue.

　　And don't leave planks unplaned when you construct a home, for you

　　Will bring a crow upon the house to caw an evil fate.

　　From pots that are unsanctified, do not take food to eat

Or water for washing—these are things for which one also pays.
750 Don't place on an immobile tomb a baby of twelve days,
Or else he'll be unmanned before he reaches puberty;
And even with a twelve-year old the same thing still might be.
Do not make use of water from a woman's bath to clean
Your own male body—such an act could easily be your bane.
755 And do not, if you come upon a blazing sacrifice,
756 Find fault with things unseen—for this, the god exacts a price.
760   Flee from the craven rumor, if you're wise, of wretched men;
For rumor is an evil—insubstantial, light, and vain,
Easy to raise but hard to bear, and hard to put aside.
Of all the rumors ever spread, not one has ever died
Completely; she herself's a kind of goddess, as you see.
765   The days are sent from Zeus, so mark them well, attentively;
And tell your slaves the thirtieth is the month's best-suited day
To oversee the work and portion out the food supply—
When people judge correctly and observe it as it is.
The days ordained by Zeus, the ingenious counselor, are these:
770 The first and fourth and seventh days are holy days to men
(Apollo of the golden sword was born from Leto then—
Upon this last), the eighth and ninth as well. Moreover, two
Days of the waxing month stand out for tasks men have to do,
The eleventh and the twelfth—those days are excellent indeed
775 For shearing sheep or gathering up the corn that makes men glad;
And yet the twelfth is better than the eleventh, it is said,
For on that day the upward-floating spider spins its thread
At noon—the time the Provident piles up its little home:
A woman should set to work upon that day and ply her loom.
780   The thirteenth of the waxing month is a day that you should shun
For sowing, but for planting vines there is no better one.
For planting vines the middle sixth is uncongenial but
Good for the birth of males—although for females it is not

Suited, and especially not for taking a marriage vow.
785 While the first sixth isn't suited for the birth of girls (although
786 For gelding kids it's kind, or building pens to enclose the herds),
788 It's fine for the birth of boys—though they'll be prone to utter words
789 That mock and lie and wheedle and in secret whispers coax.
790 Geld your boar on the eighth of the month and the loud-bellowing ox,
And on the twelfth day of the month the long-laboring mule.
On the great twentieth day beget, when the day is full,
A son; for he'll be wise and have a deep and complex mind.
The tenth is good for the birth of boys; and for a girl you'll find
795 The middle fourth, which is a day to soothe and gently tame
The sheep and curved-horned, shambling kine by laying hands on them,
The sharp-toothed dog and laboring mule. But guard against the pains
And griefs that gripe you on the month's fourth day, both when it wanes
And when it waxes: it's a day that's sacred to each god.
800 On the fourth day of the month bring back a wife to your abode,
When you have judged which birds of omen serve best for this deed.
But shun the fifth day—fifth days are both difficult and dread;
For on the fifth the Furies were attendant on the scene
When Oath was born to Strife to give to perjurers their bane.
805 Upon the middle seventh throw Demeter's holy grain
Onto the rounded threshing floor as carefully as you can,
And have the woodsman cut the planks to build a house, and lots
Of timbers that will fit together neatly for the boats;
And on the fourth the long and narrow boats can be begun.
810 The middle ninth is better when it's past the afternoon;
The first ninth, though, for human beings, is harmless, quite benign—
For planting and for being born; indeed, it's very fine
For men and women both; this day is never bad all through.
And yet, the third ninth's best of all, though this is known by few—
815 Best to start in on a jar, and also best to put
The yoke on mules and oxen and on horses fleet of foot,

And draw the ship with many benches down to the wine-dark sea;
But there are few who speak of it as it is meant to be.
Open a jar on the middle fourth—the day that's holiest.
820   Again, few know the after-twentieth day of the month is best
At dawn and that it worsens when the sun sinks in the west.
To those who live on earth, these are the days that are most blessed;
The others are indifferent, have no character or fate:
Though one man praises this one and another praises that,
825   A day can be a mother or stepmother—it depends.
How fortunate and blessed is he who all this comprehends,
Who blamelessly performs his work before the deathless ones,
And always judging birds of omen, all transgressions shuns.

NOTES

THESE NOTES ARE MEANT TO FACILITATE EASY READING AND TO PROVIDE the curious with extra information about some details of the poems. For greater depth and understanding on topics relating to mythology, sociology, and history pertaining to Hesiod's poems, the works listed as references are excellent resources. M. L. West's two commentaries on the *Theogony* and the *Works and Days* are profound, entertaining, and comprehensive treasures from which the reader without Greek can still profit greatly.

THEOGONY

1–115 Hesiod's invocation to the Heliconian Muses is the longest and most distinctive invocation in ancient epic. Helicon is the largest mountain in Boeotia, and Hesiod's home town, Ascra (*WD* 639), was on one of its slopes.

The proem (opening lines of the poem) can be divided into three sections, each of which represents a new beginning: lines 1–35, 36–103, and 104–115.

11 "aegis-bearing": an epithet of Zeus; the aegis, a goat-skin cloak or shield, was viewed as ageless and immortal, and thus as conferring protection from attack. Athena gives her aegis to Achilles in Homer's *Iliad* to frighten the Trojans.

26–28 See the general introduction on the unreliability of the Muses in Hesiod's proem in the *Theogony,* in contrast to the clarity of the invocation to the Muses in the *Works and Days*.

35 "tree or rock": the allusion is obscure, but the speculations of scholars are rich, plausible, and entertaining; for details, see West. Suggestions include a reference in Plato's *Phaedrus* (275b-c) to wisdom that comes from tree or rock, and to the story that the first poet, Orpheus, could make the trees and rocks listen to him.

53 Mnemosyne: her name is the Greek word for "memory," and as the mother of the Muses she is seen as one of the Muses herself and, hence, like them, a goddess. Memory is the great skill that singers need in order to perform, but the irony that forgetfulness is, for humans, the great benefit of song is not lost on Hesiod.

Pieria, where the Muses were born, is immediately to the north of Olympos; the Muses are called "Pierian," as well as "Olympian," which Hesiod explains in line 62.

56–60 Commonly in myth, the number of children is the outcome of the number of sexual meetings.

64 "Graces and Desire": *Charites* and *Himeros,* goddesses personifying these qualities.

81–92 The combination of the favor of Zeus and the Muses gives men wisdom and persuasion; this is what kings ought to be (88), not what they are in the *Works and Days.* For the role of kings as arbiters, see the note to *WD* line 38. Kings, the representatives of Zeus's justice on earth, need the Muses for speech that will enact justice.

116 Chasm: the word in Greek is *chaos.* The English word "chaos" comes from the Greek but has taken on a different meaning. The Greek word means "empty space" or "abyss" and is closer to our "chasm."

117 "eternal ground": the Greek word *hedos* means seat, or foundation. The translation "eternal ground" puns on the sense in which not only is Gaia the Earth and the literal ground, but all of the other gods are grounded in (and on) her.

119 Tartaros is here personified, though it is generally a place, not a god.

139 The Kyklopes of Homer's *Odyssey,* and of the later tradition, are quite unlike these "one-eyed craftsmen who made Zeus's thunderbolts in gratitude for their release (501–6)" (West). Kyklops means "circle-eye," and we have retained the transliteration of the Greek "k" sound as more authentic, despite English-speakers' greater familiarity with the "s" sound of "Cyclops."

156 Ouranos blocks the birth of his children by forcing them back inside the Earth, their mother. Kronos will swallow his children, likewise to prevent the inevitable usurpation by the next generation. Zeus will swallow his wife.

169 Kronos's speech to his mother, Gaia, marks the beginning of the cycle of usurpations involving the three generations of gods, a cycle that ends with Zeus. Gaia has made the weapon for Ouranos's castration from her own stores of metal, and she helps her son (and then her grandson Zeus, lines 479 and 494) in the overthrowing of the tyrannical parent. Her original power to generate life without a male, however, is eventually appropriated by the offspring she has assisted.

185 Erinyes: the Furies; the role that these chthonic deities play as avengers of family crimes is reasonably explained by their birth out of this crime of a son against his father.

197–99 Aphrodite's different appellations (the Greek word for foam is *aphros,* as the translation indicates): "Kytherea," for the place with which she is associated, like "the Galilean" for Jesus; and "Kyprogenia," *Kypris* (the island of Cyprus, which was devoted to the goddess) with *geneia,* associated with birth; in other words, "born from Cyprus."

208 "Called them Titans (Strainers) on account of all their straining": The name "Titan" is linked to a verb that means "to strain" or "stretch," and Hesiod is pointing this out. Interestingly the name "Israel," which Jacob is given after he wrestles with the angel in the Genesis story, also means "he who strains" or "he who strives with."

215 Hesperides: daughters of Hesperus, the Evening, they are known for tending the golden apples and for their sweet singing. Herakles had to get some of their apples as one of his labors.

223 Nemesis: in Homer *nemesis* is not associated with the gods; see note on *WD* 200, where it is associated with *aidos,* shame.

224–32 The children of Night (224–25) and the children of Strife (226–32) are abstract nouns personified.

231–32 Oath, the last of Strife's children, is presented here as harmful because of the way men use her when they make a false oath. In origin, an oath is a form of curse that one places on oneself if what one says is false.

235 "nary an error": Hesiod makes wordplay with the first syllable of Nereus's name and the sound of the Greek adjective *nemertes* describing him, an adjective that means *unerring* or infallible.

267 "harpies with lovely hair": these lovely female monsters, perhaps in origin spirits of the winds, seize people and carry them off forever. They have not here developed into the foul-smelling harpies of the third book of Vergil's *Aeneid.*

278 "the dark-haired sea god": epithet for Poseidon.

281–83 Hesiod supplies etymologies for the name of Pegasus, the horse who sprang from springs, Greek *pegai,* and for Chrysaor, the hero whose name means "golden sword."

"Chrysaor" is variously pronounced in this translation according to the requirements of the meter: in line 281 the accent is on the penultimate syllable, Chry-sá- or; in 283 it is on the antepenultimate syllable, Chrý-sa-or.

301 The "she" here is ambiguous; the reference is either to the Echidna or to Keto.

306 Typhon: the same figure as the monster Typhoeus, who is described in line 821 f.

384–85 the children of Styx: Victory is the goddess *Nike;* Glory, *Zelos,* is here not *Kleos,* the epic gift of glory in battle and the fame won for it, but the glory of successful emulation or rivalry, the dark counterpart of which is Envy (see *WD* 195).

"Power and Strength": both words for concrete strength personified as divinities; *Kratos* is power, with connotations tending toward rule, force, and domination; *Bia* is force, strength, often violence or an act of violence (see note on *WD* 213).

400 "And made her the great oath by which the Olympian gods all swear": Styx is the goddess by whom the gods swear a binding oath, the equivalent to Oath for humans. When the gods swear by Styx they also make a libation (pour a liquid as part of a sacrifice) with her water. Like Oath, Styx invokes a curse upon one who swears falsely.

406 Leto is best known for her children, Apollo and Artemis. Apollo's birth is told in the Homeric *Hymn to Apollo.*

409–52 This passage is sometimes referred to as a hymn to Hekate. She and her cult are thought to have a family connection to Hesiod. This account is a near-unique ancient instance of the disclosure of personal beliefs about a god. Mostly we see Greek gods in terms of a pantheon, and in the *Theogony* it is particularly important to set out how the different gods received their due place and honors (their *timē,* in the parlance of Greek epic) and how Zeus achieved order among the competing deities. Thus the gods are pigeon-holed in a way that could not have been characteristic of their function in the actual setting of their worshipers. Hesiod's account of Hekate by contrast portrays a goddess through the eyes of a devotee, and we see something more of the role that a local god might play. It seems from this narrative that her powers are diverse, meet the needs of her worshipers, and are happily tolerated by the other gods. She is also a very far cry from the later version of this goddess who crept though Roman sources to Shakespeare and has grim associations with the night and with unnatural, uncivilized behaviors generally. This dark and scary Hekate is perhaps born of her chthonic associations, though the only realm in Hesiod's account that she does not touch is Tartaros. West calls Hesiod "Hekate's evangelist" here.

484 "Aegean mountain": the specific reference is unidentifiable.

499 Pytho: the site of the Delphic oracle. The stone was still being shown at Delphi in the second century CE.

501 "his father's brothers": this refers to the Kyklopes; see line 139.

522 There is some ambiguity on how Prometheus is chained to the pillar. Some artistic evidence from vases represents Prometheus impaled on the pillar; in Hesiod's version the chains are driven through the pillar and then bind Prometheus.

527–30 "that foul affliction": Zeus permits Herakles to kill the eagle for the sake of the fame his son will gain from destroying a formidable menace, but it does not say that he frees Prometheus from his bonds.

535 Mekone: the remarkable idea that gods and men once lived together goes unremarked by Hesiod. The account that follows, of Prometheus's trick with the sacrificial meats, tells of our separation from the gods and gives the explanation for why sacrifices are practiced as they are.

538–41 The nutritious, meaty, bloody parts are wrapped in tripe, stomach lining, which makes those pieces look unpleasant; the fatty wrapping for the bones has no food value but looks tasty.

556–57 In the ritual of sacrifice the gods receive the sweet-smelling smoke that rises up to heaven; in our separate but shared meal, we must eat the meat, since we are mortal.

551 Hesiod attempts to protect us from the inference that Zeus was deceived, but he must have been.

559 This line is identical to *Works and Days,* line 54.

563–69 Another volley exchanged: Zeus keeps fire from humans but Prometheus uses the fennel stalk to hide a spark. Fire allows for civilization (cooked food) and technology (metal work).

572 Zeus takes the final round, and in return for the gift of fire he has Hephaistos design the evil for men, in the likeness of a maid—though if she is the first, one wonders how he found the likeness. The story of the first woman's creation is told again in more and different detail, and earlier in the poem, in the *Works and Days,* where she has a name.

578–84 The description of the golden crown that Hephaistos, the great metal-worker, fashions is an example of ekphrasis, a literary mode in which an artistic work is depicted in words and in which the depiction often contains more than an actual object of art could represent. Parallels are the shield of Achilles in Homer's *Iliad,* the temple to Apollo in book six of Vergil's *Aeneid,* or the divinely sculptured pavement in Dante's *Purgatorio.* The marvel of the crown, with its beasts of land and sea that seem to be alive and have voices, is an echo of the wonder that the woman is to man and god alike (line 588). She and the crown are both works of art.

592–612 "Poverty" is the same word in Greek as "Hunger" (*WD* 299, 301) and "Want" (*WD* 496). Women in their husbands' houses are like the drones in the beehive; they are idle and only consume, staying inside. Hesiod uses the same metaphor of drones to describe men who do no work in the *Works and Days,* lines 303–5. The best a man can hope for is a wife who will store things; heterosexual reproduction is the price of fire.

722–28 The Titans' fall to Tartaros: the number nine is three times the important number three; the brazen wall, with night poured around the neck, seems to imagine Tartaros as a large storage vessel.

734 Obriareos, an alternative name for Briareos, is one of Zeus's hundred-handed uncles.

736–40 Tartaros is ambiguously conceived, both as the place where the roots of a world tree has its roots (cf. 728) and as a vast emptiness.

744, 746 Lower-case "chasm" is distinguished from the state of the cosmos— "Chasm," personified as a goddess—before the creation of Earth (Gaia); see line 177.

767–69 "the chthonian god": Hades, unnamed here along with his guardian hound Kerberos, so as to provide greater emphasis.

777–79 The house of Styx is somewhat difficult to envision.

784–85 Iris's golden jug (standard material for a divine accoutrement) may be the source for the popular myth associating Iris with the rainbow.

819 Kymopolea: mentioned only here in extant Greek literature; her name means "Wave-Walker."

821–80: defeat of Typhoeus: he is Gaia's last child, and he poses the final challenge by a chthonic deity to the dominance of the sky god Zeus.

822 Tartaros is here a person, as in line 119; elsewhere it is a place.

831–35 The various voices suggest an antecedent myth in which Typhoeus actually metamorphosed into different animals.

886–900 Metis's name is the Greek word for "cunning," "wisdom," and "resource" (it is the hallmark trait of Homer's Odysseus). Zeus ingests her and takes the last action in the cycle of swallowing and blocking initiated by his grandfather Ouranos. By doing so he takes into himself her wisdom, and he prevents her from bearing a son who would repeat the challenge he himself posed to Kronos. The daughter she is pregnant with, Athena, is born out of Zeus's own head, and thus he also absorbs into himself the potent force of female reproductivity. Note that this is done on the advice of Gaia.

895 "Tritogeneia": epithet for Athena, taken to mean by Hesiod "born for three"—that is, for her mother, her unconceived brother, and herself.

901–3 The Horae are goddesses of the seasons and are associated with agriculture, human productive labors (the *erga* of the *Works and Days*), and fertility, both human and agricultural. Here, however, Hesiod personifies them as civic attributes—Good Order (*Eunomia*), Justice (*Dike*), and Peace (*Eirene*). West notes that all along the prosperity of men's *erga* (works) depended on civil justice.

925 Atrytone: "the Unwearied," an epithet for Athena only here and in Homer.

951 "an end to all his labors": labors mentioned throughout the *Theogony;* see lines 287–335. The myth of Herakles's deification is late, and both Homer and Hesiod ignore it.

963 Hesiod here bids farewell to the Olympian gods, with whom his Muses begin their song (see line 114).

992 This line is catalectic in the Greek—that is, it is missing the first syllable.

1021–22 The poem is thought to end at line 1020, and these two lines serve as a link to what came next and is now lost, the *Catalog of Women*. The poem we have by that name is certainly not Hesiod's.

References

Clay, J. S. 2003. *Hesiod's Cosmos*. Cambridge: Cambridge University Press.
Hamilton, Richard. 1981. *Hesiod's* Theogony. Bryn Mawr, PA: Bryn Mawr College.
The Oxford Classical Dictionary, 3rd. ed. 1996. Ed. Simon Hornblower and Antony Spawforth. Oxford: Oxford University Press.
West, Martin L. 1966. *Hesiod:* Theogony. Oxford: Clarendon Press.

WORKS AND DAYS: NOTES

1–10 The proem, or opening lines of the poem, make a double invocation to the Muses and to Zeus (line 9). It also becomes clear in line 10 that the poem's addressee is the poet's brother Perses. Thus, there is a triple speech act in the opening lines: the invocation to the Muses and to Zeus, and the address to Hesiod's brother. The address to Perses reveals that Zeus's justice in this poem is clearly involved with human life on earth.

9 "straighten": the idea embodied in the metaphor of "straightness" and "straightening" is very important in the ancient Greek concept of justice, down through Athenian democratic practices. See, for example, line 261 on the harm done by "bent" judgments.

11 Strife: *Eris* in Greek, which means the impulse that gives rise to war (personified here as Discord may be in English), the strife of war itself, or more generally a quarrel, strife, or struggle. Hesiod exploits a secondary, more positive sense of the word that means contention or contest, competitive struggle that leads to excellence, and he contrasts it to the first sense of the word.

38 "gift-eating kings": Hesiod depicts an era in Greece of ongoing political changes that in the late sixth century would result in the organization of *poleis*—what we call city-states—around Greece and the Peloponnesus. Ruling classes of kings—*basileis,* the tribal chieftains of the sort Agamemnon and Achilles represent in Homer's *Iliad*—controlled the local distribution of wealth and power. In Hesiod's account the "gift-eating kings," acting as legal arbiters, took bribes from his brother Perses.

40–41 This counterintuitive assertion, that the half is better than the whole, has drawn much attention from readers. It poses the same challenge to human life with which the poem as a whole struggles, that, as mortals, we cannot have the easy life of the gods, and that given this reality the whole is a portion beyond justice for us.

Mallow and asphodel are nutritionally inferior plants that were eaten by the poor.

The reference to "fools" who fail to grasp such evident wisdom, and Hesiod's periodic address to his brother Perses as a "fool," are habits of the didactic genre to heighten the speaker's authority.

45 The steering oar of a boat is stored above the fireplace when not in use.

48 Prometheus: his name means "forethought"; his brother is named Epimetheus, "afterthought." The word root *-met-* or *-med-* "thought" or "cunning" is found also in the name of Zeus's first wife, Metis (*Theogony* 886).

59 Zeus's hostility to humans, and that of the Greek gods generally, contrasts starkly with the modern Christian notion of a divine figure.

60–81 Pandora's manufacture. Note the convention of the narrative (a pattern typical of ancient narratives) whereby the text relates Zeus's specific orders for Pandora's production (59–69), and then repeats much of it in describing the execution of the orders (70–79). The first woman's name is a simple identity name; "pan" means "all" and "dora" means "gifts": Pandora is the gift to men from *all* the gods; she can also be construed as one gifted by all the gods, possessing all their gifts.

68 "Hermes, slayer of dogs": *Argeiphontes* is an epithet for Hermes, the meaning of which is obscure; "dog slayer," from Hermes's murder of the multi-eyed watchdog Argos, is one suggestion.

83–89 The aptly named Epimetheus (Afterthought) takes Pandora, though his brother Prometheus had warned him not to do so.

94–99 When the sixteenth-century Dutch humanist Erasmus translated these lines he confused the Greek word for jar, *pithos,* with the word for box, *pyxos;* hence our commonplace, "opening Pandora's box." In a sense "box," as the all-purpose storage container of the modern world and thus equivalent to the ancient *pithos,* does make more sense for us; but "box" loses important elements of the Greek word that make the jar, rounded in shape and made of clay, a metonymy for Pandora herself. The hope remaining inside the jar is the man's offspring, contained inside the woman's body and about which he can have very little certainty. In line 97 in Greek the word "inside" is the first word and "outside" the last word, so that the syntax helps the listener hear the structural problem of inside and outside.

106 Transition to the myth of metals, Hesiod's second explanation (Pandora being the first one) of why we humans must work. The myth of the five races is thought to have roots in Mesopotamia; compare the story of Nebuchadnezzar's dream in the Bible's book of Daniel 2:33f.

107 "How, from a single origin, mortals and gods are sprung": Hesiod does not proceed to tell how mortals and gods sprang from a single origin: he tells of the different races of men. In the *Theogony* Hesiod tells how the cosmos, including the gods, comes from "chasm"; this word is our word "chaos," but it means "empty space," "abyss," rather than "disorder."

The Olympian deities make the races of gold and silver; Zeus himself makes the bronze race and the heroes; but Hesiod mentions no maker for the iron race.

111 Golden age: Kronos's time as king (though this is not recounted in the *Theogony*) is traditionally the golden age for humans, before the overthrow of his father by Zeus. Accounts of this idyllic time regularly tell how humans did not need to work, how food grew uncultivated from the earth, and how humans lived harmoniously with the rest of the creatures of the earth. In the Roman tradition (e.g., Vergil's *Aeneid* and Ovid's *Metamorphoses*), Saturn, the equivalent or calque of Kronos, presided over the golden age in Latium.

122 The souls of the men of the golden age become guardian spirits—tutelary deities, or *daimones*—spirits loosely connected to the divine, though not strictly gods themselves. Socrates's famous inward monitor in Plato's *Apology* and elsewhere has, or is, a voice linked to this power and is called a *daimonion*.

174 The race of iron, the fifth: Zeus will eradicate this race too. To this race the children will be born gray at the temples, that is, born old; their mortality is exaggerated as death is near at the very start of life. The first-person address here is arresting.

195 Envy: personified, as Strife is, and thus having a sort of superhuman power.

197–201 The abstract nouns Restraint and Censure are described and personified by Hesiod first in terms of their bodies, before he identifies them explicitly.

200 Restraint: Greek *aidos,* which can be translated as "decency," or, related to its basic meaning of "shrinking back," as "restraint," is a complement to Justice; it is also translated as "shame." Censure: Greek *Nemesis* means "public disapproval" and properly is related to the word's basic idea of distribution or apportionment of what is due. The two abstract nouns are frequently paired. *Nemesis* only later on becomes identified with the "spirit of fateful revenge" (Verdenius).

202–12 The fable of the hawk and the nightingale: this is a grim story of *realpolitik,* involving the powerful and the innocent, whose moral of force and domination is the model of justice Perses is presumably meant to reject.

213 Greek has two words that we translate as "violence." One is *hubris,* which in English has come to connote a dangerous degree of arrogance, but in its original meaning has the sense of "overstepping one's limits" and encroaching on the domain of another, and so is the opposite of justice; "violence" in this sense gives the idea of violation. The other word is *bia,* which, connoting physical strength, force, or an act of violence, is less likely to be metaphorical violence than *hubris* (see line 275).

214 "for the man of little consequence": the view of justice, consistent with the fable, is in this passage pragmatic; the low man on the totem pole cannot afford violent or outrageous behavior—it is hard enough for the man of stature to sustain.

219–20 Oath and Justice: see *Theogony* 231; Oath here is personified to the point of being a god.

225–37 Those who observe straight justice, Hesiod suggests, will reap the benefits of a well-ordered *polis,* tantamount to a second golden age. Children who resemble their fathers (line 235) are born to women who have stayed inside the house; that is, the just man will not have to endure the anxiety that Pandora prompts about the paternity of his children.

236 For Hesiod, sailing is a dangerous and unpleasant activity, as he will say later in this poem (see line 682).

256 Justice (*Dike*) and the Muses, daughters of Zeus, are the only divine figures (discounting Hermes and Hercules) who can dwell both among mortals on earth and with the Olympians. In Hesiod's cosmos the boundaries between the spheres of Sky (Heaven), Earth, and the Underworld are firm.

263 "Straighten your utterances": see the proem, line 9, and the explicit connections in the *Theogony* among Justice, the Muses, and speech.

301 Hunger: the abstract noun personified, as a companion.

304 "stingless drones": here the drones are lazy men who do no work and consume the work of industrious men, the bees. In *Theogony* 594–99 the drones, contrary to sexual entomology that Hesiod doubtless knew, were females, consuming the work of bees.

317 Restraint is not here personified, whereas in line 324 Shame and Shamelessness are again given the attributes of personal agency.

335 "witless": Again, castigating the stupid lends vigor to the speaker of the didactic genre.

356 "Giving is good but Seizing bad": Hesiod's personified abstractions in this aphoristic line are as odd in the Greek as in English.

373–74 The woman is first described in terms of her sexual appeal. The curious word that describes her, *pugostolos*—the meaning of which is not entirely clear and may mean "swivel-hipped" or the like—is clearly an alluring trait, which is the problem for the man. She is second described in terms of her speech, and Hesiod uses the same word that describes Pandora's wheedling speech in line 78. Like the woman of the *Theogony,* she is an eater of the household's goods, from the inside.

383 Pleiades: the constellation, the rising of which is a marker for when to plant, sow, and reap.

391 "naked, plow": the reason for this odd injunction to be naked when sowing and plowing is unclear. Perhaps these activities are best done when it is warm enough to do them without clothing; perhaps garments get in the way.

417 "the dog star Sirius": the Greeks marked as the hottest day of the year the time when the star Sirius rises in the daytime, July 19. Its heat was thought to contribute to the sun's heat when Sirius shone in the daytime sky, making July and August the hottest months, and in Greek and Latin poetry it becomes a ubiquitous metonymy for the destructive heat of summer. Sirius, the dog star, similarly gives us the "dog days" of summer.

423–33 One plow is man-made; the other, the nature-made plow, has a plow-tree made from a piece of wood found bent.

"Athena's slave": a specialist in this kind of artisan labor, a joiner.

437–47 The instructions for choosing oxen and men follow the same rationale. Both the man and the bull, if too young, will be overly involved with their companions and thus less useful to their master.

448 "crane's voice": the cry of the crane, flying toward Africa, was taken as a signal of autumn (see Homer *Iliad,* 3.4).

464–65 Hades, hostile to growth, is propitiated by a field that lies fallow. Chthonian Zeus is operating in the earth, not in the sky; his character is ambiguous, as West notes, either an extension of Zeus or a separate, chthonic (i.e., earthly) counterpart of the sky-Zeus.

486 The song of the cuckoo is a harbinger of spring.

496 Want and Hardship: often paired in Greek. Hardship: "want of resources," "helplessness"; Want: "poverty." Want, or *penia,* is the mother of Eros, according to Socrates in Plato's *Symposium.*

500 Hope: the ambivalence of hope in the Greek mind is evident here, just as in the story of Pandora's jar.

504–5 "oxen-flaying days": West says the days are cold and windy enough "to take the hide off an ox."

January: the Greek month *Lenaion;* this is our earliest written instance of the name of a Greek month.

507 "horse-nurturing Thrace": Thrace (the Balkan peninsula south of the Danube, modern Bulgaria, and parts of Greece and Turkey) is flat country, thus ideal for raising horses; the wind whips across it.

519–25 A very odd pairing of the images of the young girl, whom the narrative casts in an erotic light, and the octopus. Both are in retreat, the girl deep inside the house with her mother, the octopus hidden deep in the dark sea. The "boneless one" is an instance of a kenning, in which a metaphorical expression is substituted for the concrete name of a thing.

536–46 Hesiod's instructions for dressing in winter, like his instructions on making a plow, have a precision characteristic of epic descriptions of a process; compare Odysseus's meticulous construction of the raft in *Odyssey* 5.244f.

559–71 The longer nights mean longer sleeping, which means less eating, so that the farmer can save on rations for his men and animals.

565 Arcturus: the brightest star in the Bear constellation; used for navigation.

568 "daughter of Pandion": the swallow. Philomela is Pandion's daughter; she and her sister Procne were turned into swallows, or, in Ovid *Metamorphoses* 6, into nightingales.

571 "he-who-carries-his-own-house": the snail, another example of a kenning (see line 524).

589 "wine from Biblos": good wine, possibly from the region of Biblos in Thrace; but the reference is obscure.

633–60 The unusual inclusion of personal material (here, and throughout in the depiction of the conflict with Perses) has given readers a biography for Hesiod, though some of it should no doubt be attributed to the artistic posture Hesiod adopts in this poem.

654–59 Hesiod won first prize in a singing contest at the funeral games for Amphidamus, put on by his sons. Some suggest that the song he sang was the *Theogony*.

657 "tripod": a three-legged utensil of any kind, but especially one designed to hold a cauldron used for boiling meat; some of these cauldrons had the three legs attached. Such tripods had great value; they came to be associated with their role of cooking meat in sacrificial contexts and hence became themselves suitable as gifts dedicated to the gods; they were also awarded as prizes in contests.

682–91 Hesiod's antipathy to sailing is not unreasonable: Greek ships did not have rudders, the seas are unpredictable, and navigation was seat-of-the-pants by the stars.

733 See the book of Leviticus 15.16–18 for prohibitions of a similar nature to this one; idea reminiscent of this section of the *Works and Days* can be found throughout Leviticus. West notes that sexual intercourse "is widely held to impair ritual purity."

765–827 *The Days:* Like a good deal else in Hesiod's poems, this section has seemed to some scholars, for various reasons, to be written by someone besides Hesiod. The ancient evidence however is with Hesiod. In the poem up to this point, time is counted according to astronomical and seasonal phenomena. This section marks time by the lunar calendar, which, as West points out, would have worked in tandem with other time markers. Readers curious about the details of Hesiod's calendar and ways of counting days should consult West's commentary, but one can be instructed and intrigued by these verses without specialized knowledge. The idea that days are auspicious or inauspicious for certain important human activities, and that those days are measured by the waxing and waning moon, is universal and as old as time. And, despite prim accusations that this kind of thinking is "irrational," nevertheless an attempt to order, divide, and classify what Aldous Huxley called the "terrifying undifferentiated span of time" that stretches out before us seems full of reason.

Overgeneralizing a bit, there are three methods of counting at work here: taking the whole month inclusively, e.g., 766, "the thirtieth"; dividing the month into a waxing and waning half, e.g., 780, "the thirteenth"; dividing the month into thirds of decads (ten-day period), e.g., 782, "the middle sixth," which would be the sixteenth in our counting.

765 "the days sent are from Zeus": the characteristics of the days are in accordance with divine will.

778 "the Provident": a kenning, probably for the ant.

786 and 787 are combined into one line: the texts are not corrupt here, but the translation into English, in a rare instance, needed less verbal space than the Greek; nothing substantive has been omitted by the translation.

789 The boy born on the first sixth of the month will have words that "mock and lie and wheedle," which is the same phrase that describes the speech Hermes gives to Pandora in line 78.

802–4: The Furies exact punishments from those who swear falsely; Oath, the act of swearing, is personified as a deity (see line 219); Strife: the same figure with whom Hesiod began, the bad kind of *Eris* (see lines 14 and 28). Some readers observe that the waxing half of the month is best, and in fact the fifth is the only unequivocally awful day in the first half, according to Hesiod.

815 "start in on a jar" and **819:** open a fresh container on this day (the third ninth, or the twenty-ninth of the month); the container is a *pithos*. What it contains seems not to matter.

820–21 Days themselves can be divided in half (also in 810).

References

Tandy, David W., and Walter C. Neale. 1996. *Hesiod's* Works and Days: *A Translation and Commentary for the Social Sciences.* Berkeley: University of California Press.

Verdenius, W. J. 1985. *A Commentary on Hesiod:* Works and Days, vv. 1–382. Leiden: E. J. Brill.

West, Martin L., editor and commentator. 1978. *Hesiod: Works and Days.* Oxford: Clarendon Press.

GLOSSARY

NOTES ON THE GLOSSARY

THE MAJORITY OF NAMES AND PHRASES CONTAINED IN THIS GLOSSARY ARE Greek. Where the English equivalent rather than the Greek term is given in the translation, however, it is the English term that is glossed. An example is Strife, the Greek *Eris* (on which Hesiod focuses at the beginning of the *Works and Days*). If both the Greek term and its English equivalent are given in the translation (e.g., *Okeanos* and Ocean), it is the Greek term that is glossed. Line references usually pertain to the Greek names, but in some cases they apply to their English equivalents as well.

In the transliteration of Greek names, we have generally tried to follow the Greek pronunciation and orthography rather than the Latin equivalent; thus, Akhilleus rather than Achilles. Greek names are often familiar in their Latinized versions, however, and therefore we thought that it would be better to retain the familiar spellings in some cases than to preserve complete consistency. Thus, Helicon is given with the Latinate "c" rather than the Greek "k." But because this is a poetic translation, tonal and rhythmic considerations have taken precedence; thus, for the sake of the sound, Akhilleus rather than Achilles, even though the latter is the more familiar form.

Like translation, the process of transliterating and pronouncing Greek names in English is an uneven procedure, and countervailing forces affect the outcome of deriving the English name from the Greek. Our first goal in providing this glossary is to give the reader a guide for making the verse of our translation readable out loud, a poem that is spoken (and heard), if not sung as the original was. Beyond that, we have made compromises between what is currently thought to be an accurate pronunciation of Greek and the tradition in English that has made these names part of our literary inheritance. We judged that it is absurd to insist on pronouncing Poseidon as "posādon"— though the -ei- diphthong that is transliterated out of the Greek is generally pronounced like a long "a" in English (as in "tape"), but reasonable to suggest the pronunciation of Peitho (the goddess Persuasion) as "pāthō"; we suggest Eirene as "ārēnē," though the latter has come into English as the woman's name "Irene." We have occasionally made some arbitrary, meter-driven choices; the name Chrysaor, for instance, takes the accent on the middle syllable, except that at *Theogony* line 283 the meter finds it convenient to put the accent on the first syllable.

The phonetic equivalents are those used in the pronunciation key of the *American Heritage Dictionary,* with some minor alterations.

Greek sounds in the English text represented by	phonetic equivalents	phonetic pronunciation
a	ə	about
a	ä	father
a	a	pat
a	ā	pay
ae	ā	pay
ai	ī	bite
ae	ī	bite
au	ou	out
e	ē	meet
e	e	pet
e(r)	â	care
e	ə	item
eu	yoo	yew
eus	ā-əs	truce
i	ī	bite
i	i	bit
y	i	bit
y	oo	boot [Euphrosyne]
o	o	pot
o	ō	toes

o	ə	gall<u>o</u>p
oi	oi	n<u>oi</u>se
u	u	c<u>u</u>t
u	ə	circ<u>u</u>s
ur	ûr	<u>ur</u>ge
ou	oo	b<u>oo</u>t

The stress marks (ˈ) indicate which syllable is accented.

GLOSSARY OF NAMES AND PHRASES

Achaians (ə-khīˈ-əns): a collective term for all Greeks (*WD* 652)

Acheloüs (a-khe-lōˈ-əs): one of the rivers that Tethys bore to Okeanos (*Th* 340)

Actaea (ak-tāˈ-ə): a Nereid (*Th* 249)

Admete (ad-mēˈ-tē): one of the Okeanids (*Th* 349)

Aeneas (ā-nēˈ-əs): the son of Aphrodite and Anchises (*Th* 1008)

Aeolia (ā-ōˈ-lē-ə): the coast of Asia Minor colonized by Greek peoples (*WD* 636)

Aesepus (ā-sēˈ-pəs): a river (*Th* 342)

Aeson (āˈ-sən): the father of Jason (*Th* 992)

Aetna (etˈ-nə): volcanic mountain in Sicily (*Th* 860)

Aietes (ī-ēˈ-tēz): king of Iolkos and father of Medea (*Th* 957, 993)

Agave (ə-gäˈ-vā): (a) a Nereid; (b) the daughter of Kadmos and Harmonia (*Th* 247, 976)

Aglaia (ə-glīˈ-ə): one of the three Graces (Charites) (*Th* 909, 945)

Agrios (aˈ-grē-əs): son of Kirke and Odysseus (*Th* 1013)

Aidoneus (ī-do-nāˈ-əs): Hades, the god of the Underworld (*Th* 913)

Aiello (ī-elˈ-lō): one of the Harpies (*Th* 267)

Akaste (ə-käsˈ-tā): one of the Okeanids (*Th* 356)

Akhilleus (ä-khi-lāˈ-əs): the son of Thetis and Peleus (*Th* 1007)

Aldeskos (äl-desˈ-kəs): a river (*Th* 345)

Alkmene (alk-mēˈ-nē): mother of Herakles (*Th* 943, 950)

Alph (abbreviated form of Alpheos): one of the rivers that Tethys bore to Okeanos (*Th* 338)

Amphidamus (am-fi-dāˈ-məs): a king of Chalchis (*WD* 654)

Amphirho (amˈ-fi-rō): one of the Okeanids (*Th* 360)

Amphitrite (am-fi-trī'-tē): a Nereid (*Th* 243, 253, 930)

Amphitryon (am-fi'-trē-on): putative father of Herakles (*Th* 316)

Anchises (an-khī'-sēz): father of the Trojan hero Aeneus (*Th* 1009)

Apesas (ä-pe'-səs): a mountain in northeast Nemea (*Th* 331)

Aphrodite (a-frō-dī'-tē): goddess of love and beauty (*Th* 16, 196, 822, 961, 975, 980, 989, 1005, 1014; *WD* 65, 521)

Apollo (ə-pol'-lō): god of archery, music, prophecy, and healing; the epithet Phoebus means "bright" (*Th* 14, 94, 377, 919; *WD* 771)

Arcturus (ärk-tûr'-əs): a giant star in the constellation Boötes (*WD* 565, 610)

Ares (a'-rēz): god of war (*Th* 317, 922, 933, 936; *WD* 146)

Arges (är'-gās): one of the three Kyklopes (Cyclops) (*Th* 140)

Argos (är'-gos): a region in the northeast Peloponnese (*Th* 12)

Ariadne (ar-ē-ad'-nē): daughter of King Minos of Crete (*Th* 947)

Arimoi (ar'-i-moi): a people located somewhere in the east—perhaps equivalent to the Aramaeans, of ancient Syria (*Th* 304)

Aristaios (ar-is-tī'-əs): a son of Apollo (*Th* 977)

Artemis (är'-te-mis): daughter of Zeus and Leto and sister of Apollo, a goddess associated with the hunt, virginity, and childbirth (*Th* 14, 919)

Asia: one of the Okeanids (*Th* 359)

Askra (as'-krə): a town in which Hesiod tells us his father lived (*WD* 639)

Asteria (as-târ-i'-ə): the wife of Perses and mother of Hekate (*Th* 409)

Astraios (as-trī'-os): the husband of Eos; perhaps a name for the father of the stars (West) (*Th* 376, 378)

Athena (ə-thē'-nə): a goddess born from Zeus's head and associated with wisdom (*Th* 13, 318, 572, 888, 924; *WD* 64, 430)

Atlas (at'-ləs): a Titan whose task is to hold up the sky; his daughters are the Pleiades (*Th* 509, 517, 746, 938; *WD* 385)

Atropos (ə-trō'-pəs): one of the three Fates (Moirai) (*Th* 905)

Atrytone (a-trī'-tō-nē): a name given to Athena (*Th* 925)

Aulis (ou'-lis): the place where the Greek fleet assembled before sailing for Troy; on the eastern shore of Boeotia (*WD* 651)

Autonoë (ou-ton'-o-ē): (a) a Nereid; (b) daughter of Kadmos and Harmonia (*Th* 258, 977)

Badness: considered a goddess (*WD* 287)

Bellerophon (bəl-lâr'-ə-fon): a hero who had to overcome a series of ordeals (*Th* 325)

Biblos (bib'-los): a town east of Cyprus, in modern Lebanon (*WD* 589)

Boreas (bō'-rē-əs): the North Wind (*Th* 379, 870; *WD* 506, 513, 519, 547, 553)

Briareos (bri-är'-e-əs): one of the three-hundred-armed giants, born from Gaia and Ouranos, who help Zeus defeat the Titans (*Th* 149, 618, 714, 817)

Brontes (bron'-tās): one of the three Kyklopes (Cyclops); his name means "thunder" (*Th* 140)

Calliope (kə-lī'-o-pē): one of the Olympian Muses; subsequently associated with epic (*Th* 79)

Chalchis (khal'-kis): a town across the strait from Aulis (*WD* 655)

Charites (khär'-i-tās): the three Graces (*Th* 908)

Chasm: the literal meaning of the Greek Chaos; "it does not contain the idea of confusion or disorder" (West) (*Th* 116, 123, 700, 814)

Chimaera (khī-mä'-r-ə): a fire-breathing monster with three heads (*Th* 319, 321)

Chiron (khī'-ron): a centaur (*Th* 1001)

Chrysaor (khri-sā'-ōr): son of Medusa and father of Geryon (*Th* 281, 287, 980; at 283 pronounced khri'-sā-ōr)

Chrysis (kri'-sis): one of the Okeanids (*Th* 359)

Chthonian: belonging to the earth (Gaia) or to the Underworld; in general, opposed to the principle of the sky embodied by Zeus and the Olympians (*Th* 767; *WD* 464–65)

Clio (klē'-ō): one of the nine Olympian Muses; later associated with history (*Th* 77)

Clotho (klo'-thō): one of the three Fates (Moirai) (*Th* 905)

Cumae (koo'-mā): a town on the coast of Asia Minor, just south of Lesbos (*WD* 636)

Death: the god Thanatos (*Th* 212, 756, 758, 759)

Demeter (də-mē'-tûr): goddess of the harvest and of the fertility of the earth (*Th* 454, 911, 967; *WD* 32, 300, 393, 465, 598, 804)

Dike (dē'-kā): the goddess of Justice, one of the three Horae; considered the daughter of Zeus in *Works and Days* (*Th* 902; *WD* 220, 256, 275, 283)

Dione (dē-ō-nā): (a) an Olympian goddess; (b) one of the Okeanids (*Th* 17, 353)

Dionysos (dī-o-nī'-sos): the god of wine (*Th* 941, 948; *WD* 614)

Doris (dō'-ris): (a) the wife of Nereus; (b) her daughter; (c) one of the Okeanids (*Th* 241, 250, 350)

Doto (dō'-tō): a Nereid (*Th* 248)

Dynamene (doo-nä'-mə-nē): a Nereid (*Th* 248)

Echidna (ē-khid'-nə): a monster, half woman, half serpent (*Th* 297, 305)

Eileithuia (ā-lā'-thwē-ə): goddess of childbirth; daughter of Zeus and Hera (*Th* 922)

Eione (ā-ō'-nē): a Nereid (*Th* 255)

Eirene (ā-rē'-nē): the goddess of Peace, one of the three Horae (*Th* 902)

Elektra (ə-lek'-tr-ə): one of the Okeanids (*Th* 265, 349)

Eleuthera (ə-loo'-thâ-ra): a place between Boeotia and Attica (*Th* 55)

Enyo (en-ē'-ō): one of the Graiai (*Th* 273)

Eos (ā'-os): goddess of the Dawn (*Th* 19, 372, 378, 380, 451, 984; *WD* 610)

Eosphoros (ā-os'-for-os): the Morning Star (*Th* 381)

Epimetheus (e-pi-mē'-thē-əs): brother of Prometheus (the name means "afterthought") (*Th* 511; *WD* 84, 85)

Erato (e-rä'-tō): (a) one of the Olympian Muses, later associated with lyric poetry; (b) a Nereid (*Th* 77, 246)

Erebos (e'-re-bos): the realm of darkness, associated with Hades and Tartaros (*Th* 123, 125)

Eridanos (e-ri-dä'-nos): one of the rivers that Tethys bore to Okeanos (*Th* 338)

Erinyes (e-rin'-yoo-ēz): the Furies—daughters of the earth who punish family crimes, born of the blood from Ouranos's castration (*Th* 185)

Eros (e'-ros): the god of sexual love (*Th* 120, 201)

Erytheia (e-ri-thā'-ə): a mythical island, beyond the sunset, later identified with Cadiz (West) (*Th* 290, 982)

Ether: the Air personified (*Th* 124)

Euagore (yoo-ä'-gō-rä): a Nereid (*Th* 257)

Euarne (yoo-är'-nē): a Nereid (*Th* 259)

Euboea (yoo-bē'-ə): a locale in Boeotia (*WD* 651)

Eudora (yoo-dōr'-ə): (a) a Nereid born to Doris and Nereus; (b) one of the Okeanids (*Th* 244, 360)

Euenus (yoo-ē'-nəs): one of the rivers that Tethys bore to Okeanos (*Th* 345)

Eukrante (yoo-kran'-tē): a Nereid (*Th* 243)

Eulimine (yoo-lim'-i-nē): a Nereid (*Th* 247)

Eunike (yoo-nē'-kē): a Nereid (*Th* 246)

Eunomia (yoo-nō'-mē-ə): the goddess of Lawfulness, one of the three Horae (*Th* 902)

Euphrosyne (yoo-fro'-soo-nē): one of the three Graces (Charites) (*Th* 909)

Eupompe (yoo-pom'-pē): a Nereid (*Th* 261)

Europa (yûr-ō'-pə): one of the Okeanids (*Th* 357)

Euryale (yoo-rē'-ə-lā): one of the Gorgons (*Th* 276)

Eurybia (yûr-i-bē'-ə): daughter of Gaia and Pontos (*Th* 239, 375)

Eurynome (yûr-i'-nō-mē): an Okeanid, the mother of the Graces (*Th* 358, 907)

Eurytion (yûr-i'-tē-ən): cowherd killed by Herakles (*Th* 293)

Euterpe (yoo-tûr'-pē): one of the Olympian Muses, later associated with music (*Th* 77)

Furies: the Erinyes, female figures who punish crimes (*Th* 185; *WD* 802)

Gaia (gī'-ə): the goddess of the Earth (*Th* 20, 45, 106, 108, 117, 119, 126, 147, 154, 159, 173, 177, 184, 237, 421, 463, 494, 505, 626, 644, 702, 703, 821, 867, 884, 891; *WD* 32, 563)

Galatea (ga-lə-tā'-ə): a Nereid (*Th* 250)

Galaxaura (ga-ləx-our'-a): one of the Okeanids (*Th* 353)

Galena (gə-lā'-nə): a Nereid (*Th* 244)

Geryon (gâr'-ē-on): a three-headed monster killed by Herakles (*Th* 287, 289, 309, 981)

Giants: (a) a race of powerful beings, neither men nor gods (West); (b) hundred-armed figures, born from Gaia and Ouranos, who help Zeus and the Olympians defeat the Titans (*Th* 50, 185)

Glauke (glou'-kā): a Nereid (*Th* 244)

Glaukonome (glou-ko-nō'-mē): a Nereid (*Th* 256)

Gorgons: monsters with horrible faces and serpents writhing about their heads, the sight of which can turn men to stone (*Th* 274)

Graces: the Charites (*Th* 64, 908, 946)

Graiai (grī'-ī): the Old Woman born to Keto and Phorkys (*Th* 272)

Granikos (grən-ī'-kəs): one of the rivers that Tethys bore to Okeanos (*Th* 342)

Gyges (gī'-jēz): one of the three-hundred-armed giants, born from Gaia and Ouranos, who help Zeus defeat the Titans (*Th* 149, 618, 714, 734, 815)

Hades (hā'-dēz): the god of the Underworld; in other traditions, the Underworld itself and thus equivalent to Tartaros (*Th* 455, 767, 850; *WD* 153, 464)

Haliakmon (hal-ē-ak'-mon): one of the rivers that Tethys bore to Okeanos (*Th* 341)

Halimede (hal-i-mē'-dē): a Nereid (*Th* 255)

Harmonia (här-mō'-nē-ə): Harmony, the goddess of concord (*Th* 937, 975)

Harpies: goddesses of the storm-winds, who snatch people away (West) (*Th* 267)

Hebe (hē'-bē): daughter of Zeus and Hera, given as wife to Herakles (*Th* 17, 922, 951, 952)

Hekate (he'-kə-tē): daughter of Asteria and Perses, not mentioned by Homer; in Hesiod, without the sinister connotations she acquires in later traditions (West) (*Th* 411, 418, 441)

Helen: daughter of Zeus and Leda; her abduction by Paris from Menelaos precipitated the Trojan War (*WD* 166)

Helicon (hel'-i-kon): mountain in southern Boeotia where Hesiod lived (*Th* 2, 7, 23; *WD* 639, 658)

Helios (hē'-li-əs): the god of the Sun and the sun itself (*Th* 19, 371, 760, 956, 958, 1011; *WD* 536)

Hellenes (hel'-lēnz): people of Hellas, or Greece (*WD* 528)

Hephaistos (he-fīs'-tos): lame Olympian god associated with metalworking and craftsmanship; called the Dextrous One (*Th* 571, 579, 866, 928, 945; *WD* 60, 70)

Heptaporus (hep-tə-pōr'-əs): one of the rivers that Tethys bore to Okeanos (*Th* 341)

Hera (hâr'-ə): the wife of Zeus and the queen of the gods (*Th* 12, 314, 454, 921, 927, 952)

Herakles (hâr'-ə-klēz): son of Alkmene and Zeus; his exploits are alluded to in the *Theogony* (*Th* 289, 315, 332, 526, 530, 944, 950, 982)

Hermes (hûr'-mēz): the messenger god, son of Zeus and Maia (*Th* 444, 938; *WD* 68, 77)

Hermus (hâr'-məs): one of the rivers that Tethys bore to Okeanos (*Th* 343)

Hesiod (hēz'-ī-əd): the poet of the *Theogony* and the *Works and Days* (*Th* 22)

Hesperides (hes-pâr'-i-dēz): for Hesiod, the maidens who tend golden apples in a garden at the westernmost corner of the world; the word has since come to refer to that garden itself (*Th* 215, 275, 518)

Hestia (hes'-tē-ə): goddess of the hearth; child of Rhea and Kronos (*Th* 454)

Hippo (hip'-pō): one of the Okeanids (*Th* 351)

Hippocrene (hip'-pə-krēn): the "fountain of the horse," said to have been created by a kick of Pegasus's hoof (West) (*Th* 6)

Hipponoë (hip-pə-nō'-ē): a Nereid (*Th* 251)

Hippothoë (hip-pə-thō'-ē): a Nereid (*Th* 251)

Horae (hōr'-ī): the Hours; daughters of Zeus and Themis (*Th* 901; *WD* 74)

Hyades (hī'-ə-dēz): a cluster of stars in the head of the constellation Taurus (*WD* 615)

Hydra (hī'-drə): a monster with many serpent heads slain by Herakles (*Th* 313, 314)

Hyperion (hī-pēr'-i-ən): father of Helios; child of Gaia and Ouranos (*Th* 134, 374, 1011)

Ianeira (ē-ə-nâr'-ə): one of the Okeanids (*Th* 355)

Ianthe (ē-an'-thē): one of the Okeanids (*Th* 349)

Iapetos (ē-a'-pe-tos): a Titan; father of Prometheus (*Th* 18, 134, 508, 528, 543, 559, 614; *WD* 50, 54)

Iasion (ē-a'-sē-ən): a hero, or Titan, who lay with Demeter and, in some traditions, was slain by Zeus (*Th* 970)

Ida (ī'-də): a mountain in Asia Minor (*Th* 1010)

Idyia (id-wē'-ə): one of the Okeanids (*Th* 352, 960, 961)

Ilium (il'-ē-əm): another name for Troy (*WD* 653)

Íno (ī'-nō): daughter of Kadmos and Harmonia (*Th* 976)

Iolaus (ī-ō-lā'-əs): a hero who aided Herakles in killing the Hydra (*Th* 317)

Iolkos (ē-ōl'-kəs): Colchis in Thessaly, where Jason was sent to find the Golden Fleece (*Th* 997)

Íris (ī'-ris): the messenger goddess, associated with the rainbow (*Th* 266, 780, 784)

Íster (is'-tûr): one of the rivers that Tethys bore to Okeanos (*Th* 339)

Justice: Dike, the goddess of Justice (*WD* 220, 256, 275, 283)

Kadmos (kad'-məs): founder of Thebes (*Th* 326, 937, 940, 975; *WD* 163)

Kallirhoë (kal-lir'-ō-ē): one of the Okeanids (*Th* 288, 351, 979)

Kalypso (ka-lip'-sō): (a) one of the Okeanids; (b) the goddess who detained Odysseus on Ogygia (the two may or may not be the same figure) (*Th* 359, 1017)

Kephalos (kef'-ə-los): a son of Hermes (*Th* 986)

Kerberos (kûr'-bûr-əs): a fifty-headed dog who guarded Hades (*Th* 311, 769)

Kerkeis (kär-kā'-is): one of the Okeanids (*Th* 355)

Keto (kā'-tō): a sea monster (*Th* 238, 270, 333, 336)

Kirke (kir'-kē): goddess who detained Odysseus on the island of Aiaia (*Th* 957, 1011)

Klymene (klī-mē'-nē): one of the Okeanids (*Th* 351, 507)

Klytia (klī-tē-ə): one of the Okeanids (*Th* 352)

Koios (koi'-os): a Titan, sometimes associated with the planet Mercury (*Th* 133, 405)

Kottos (kot'-tos): one of the three hundred-armed giants, born from Gaia and Ouranos, who help Zeus defeat the Titans (*Th* 149, 618, 654, 714, 734, 815)

Kreios (krā'-os): a Titan, sometimes associated with the planet Mars (*Th* 133, 375)

Kronion (krō'-nē-on): Zeus, Kronos's son (*Th* 53, 534; *WD* 69, 137, 253)

Kronos (krō'-nos): son of Gaia and Ouranos, supplanted by his son, Zeus (*Th* 53, 137, 168, 395, 423, 450, 453, 459, 494, 495, 534, 572, 624, 625, 630, 634, 648, 660, 668, 851; *WD* 18, 71, 111, 158, 242, 247)

Kyklopes (ki-klo'-pās): the Cyclops (plural), three one-eyed gigantic creatures associated with thunder and lightning (*Th* 139, 144)

Kymatolege (ki-ma-to-le'-gā): a Nereid (*Th* 253)

Kymo (ki'-mō): a Nereid (*Th* 255)

Kymodoke (ki-mo-dō'-kā): a Nereid (*Th* 252)

Kymopolea (ki-mo-po-lā'-ə): daughter of Poseidon (*Th* 819)

Kymothoë (ki-mo-thō'-ē): a Nereid (*Th* 245)

Kypris (ki'-pris): the island of Cyprus, associated with and sometimes a metonymy for Aphrodite (*Th* 193, 199)

Kyprogenia (kip-ro-gān'-yə): born from Cyprus; an epithet for Aphrodite (*Th* 199)

Kythera (kith'-ər-ə): an island sacred to Aphrodite near the southeast corner of the Peloponnese (*Th* 192, 193, 198)

Kytherea (kith-ə-rē'-ə): an epithet for Aphrodite (*Th* 198, 934, 1008)

Lachesis (la-khē'-sis): one of the three Fates (Moirai) (*Th* 905)

Ladon (lä'-don): one of the rivers that Tethys bore to Okeanos (*Th* 344)

Laomedea (lā-om-ə-dē'-ə): a Nereid (*Th* 257)

Latinos (lə-tē'-nəs): son of Kirke and Odysseus (*Th* 1013)

Leagore (lā-ä'-gōr-ā): a Nereid (*Th* 257)

Lerna (lâr'-nə): a place near Argos (*Th* 314)

Leto (lē'-tō): mother of Apollo and Artemis by Zeus (*Th* 18, 406, 918; *WD* 771)

Lysianassa (li-sē-an-äs'-sə): a Nereid (*Th* 258)

Maeander (mā-an'-dûr): one of the rivers that Tethys bore to Okeanos (*Th* 339)

Maia (mī'-ə): mother of Hermes by Zeus (*Th* 938)

Medea (me-dē'-ə): daughter of Idyia by Aiëtes (*Th* 962)

Medeos (me-dā'-əs): son of Medea and Jason (*Th* 1001)

Medusa (me-doo'-sə): a Gorgon slain by Perseus (*Th* 276, 278)

Mekone (mā-kō'-nā): a place in the northeastern Peloponnese (*Th* 535)

Meliai (mel'-ē-ī): the Nymphs born to Gaia; the word means "ash trees," and so Hesiod perhaps is referring to tree-nymphs (West) (*Th* 187)

Melita (mel-ē'-tə): a Nereid (*Th* 247)

Melobosis (mel-ə-bō'-sis): one of the Okeanids (*Th* 354)

Melpomene (mel-po'-mə-nē): one of the Olympian Muses, later associated with tragedy (*Th* 77)

Memnon (mem'-non): son of Eos and Tithonos (*Th* 984)

Menestho (men-es'-thō): one of the Okeanids (*Th* 357)

Menippe (men-ip'-pē): a Nereid (*Th* 260)

Menoitios (men-oi'-ti-os): son of Klymene and Okeanos (*Th* 510, 514)

Metis (mā'-tis): one of the Okeanids, Zeus's first consort; her name means "resource" or "cunning" (*Th* 358, 886)

Minos (mī'-nos): legendary king of Crete (*Th* 947)

Mnemosyne (ne-mos'-soo-nā): Memory, mother of the Muses (*Th* 53, 135, 915)

Moirai (moi'-rī): the three Fates (*Th* 217, 904)

Muses: the goddesses who inspire poets (*Th* 1, 52, 68, 75, 94, 96, 114, 916, 965, 1021; *WD* 1, 658, 662)

Nausinoös (nou-sin'-ō-əs): son of Kalypso and Odysseus (*Th* 1018)

Nausithoös (nou-sith'-ō-əs): son of Kalypso and Odysseus (*Th* 1017)

Nemea (ne-mā'-ə): area in the northeast Peloponnese (*Th* 327, 329)

Nemertes (ne-mâr'-tēz): a Nereid (*Th* 262)

Nemesis (nem'-ə-sis): goddess of Just Resentment (*Th* 223)

Nereus (nâr'-ē-əs): a sea god, sometimes called the Old Man of the Sea (*Th* 233, 241, 263, 1003)

Nesaea (ne-sā'-ə): a Nereid (*Th* 249)

Neso (nā'-sō): a Nereid (*Th* 261)

Nessus (nes'-səs): one of the rivers that Tethys bore to Okeanos (*Th* 341)

Nile: one of the rivers that Tethys bore to Okeanos (*Th* 338)

Notos (no'-tos): god of the south wind (*Th* 380, 870)

Nux (noox): the Night (personified) (*Th* 20, 107, 123, 125, 211, 213, 223, 744, 748, 756, 758; *WD* 171)

Nymphs: (a) mountain goddesses, daughters of Gaia; (b) the Meliai, tree-nymphs (*Th* 130, 187)

Oath: Horkos, the daughter of Strife (Eris) (*Th* 231; *WD* 219, 803)

Obriareos (o-brē-är'-ē-os): another name for Briareos (*Th* 734)

Odysseus (o-dis'-sē-əs): the Homeric hero (*Th* 1012, 1017)

Oedipus (e'-di-pəs): king of Thebes (*WD* 162)

Okeanid (ō-kā-ä'-nid): daughters that Tethys bore to Okeanos (*Th* 364, 956)

Okeanos (ō-kā-ä'-nos): the god of the Ocean or the ocean personified (*Th* 20, 133, 215, 242, 265, 274, 282, 288, 337, 362, 368, 695, 776, 788, 815, 841, 907, 959, 979; *WD* 171, 566)

Okypete (ō-ki-pē'-tē): one of the Harpies (*Th* 267)

Okyrhoë (ō-kir'-ō-ē): one of the Okeanids (*Th* 360)

Olmeios (ol-mā'-əs): a stream on Mount Helicon (*Th* 6)

Olympos: the high mountain in northern Thessaly where the gods reside (*Th* 42, 62, 68, 113, 118, 391, 398, 633, 680, 689, 783, 793, 804, 842, 855, 963; *WD* 109, 127)

Orion (o-rī'-ən): the hunter constellation on the equator east of Taurus (*WD* 597, 609, 615, 620)

Orthos (or'-thos): a two-headed dog with a serpent's tail who guarded the cattle of Geryon and was killed by Herakles (*Th* 293, 309, 327)

Othrys (oth'-ris): a mountain opposite Olympos on the Thessalian plain, where the Titans had their home (*Th* 632)

Ouranos (oo'-rä-nos): the god of the Sky (*Th* 45, 106, 126, 147, 176, 207, 463, 470, 485, 501, 617, 644, 702, 891)

Pallas (pal'-ləs): (a) one of the Titans; (b) an epithet of uncertain meaning for Athena (*Th* 376, 383; *WD* 76)

Pandion (pan-dī'-ən): king of Athens, father of Procne and Philomela (*WD* 568)

Pandion's daughter: Philomela, who was turned into a swallow (*WD* 568)

Pandora (pan-dor'-ə): the woman Zeus has Hephaistos form as a punishment for Prometheus; the name means the All-Gifted One (*WD* 80)

Panope (pan'-o-pā): a Nereid (*Th* 250)

Parnassus (par-nas'-səs): a mountain northwest of Athens that was sacred to Apollo and the Muses; on its southern slope was the oracle of Apollo at Delphi (*Th* 499)

Parthenius (par-thēn'-ē-əs): one of the rivers that Tethys bore to Okeanos (*Th* 344)

Pasithea (pas-i-thā'-ə): a Nereid (*Th* 246)

Pasithoë (pa-si'-thō-ē): an Okeanid (*Th* 352)

Pegai (pe'-gī): Greek word for "springs," from which the name Pegasus is derived (*Th* 282)

Pegasus (pe'-gə-səs): the winged horse, beloved by the Muses of Mount Helicon, who helped Bellerophon overcome the Chimaera (*Th* 281, 282, 284, 325)

Peitho (pā'-thō): an Okeanid; her name means Persuasion (*Th* 349)

Peleus (pē'-lē-əs): the father by Aphrodite of Akhilleus (*Th* 1006)

Pelias (pe'-lē-əs): king of Iolkos who sent Jason to find the Golden Fleece (*Th* 996)

Pemphredo (pem-frē'-dō): one of the Graiai (*Th* 273)

Peneus (pēn'-ē-əs): one of the rivers that Tethys bore to Okeanos (*Th* 343)

Permessos (pâr-mes'-səs): a stream on Mount Helicon (*Th* 5)

Perseis (pûr-sā'-is): an Okeanid (*Th* 355, 956)

Persephone (pûr-se'-fo-nē): daughter of Demeter and Zeus and wife of Hades; she rejoins her mother in the spring and returns to her husband in the fall (*Th* 913)

Perses (pûr'-sēz): Hesiod's brother (*WD* 10, 27, 213, 274, 286, 299, 397, 611)

Perseus (pûr'-sē-əs): hero who killed the Gorgon Medusa (*Th* 280)

Petraia (pe-trī'-ə): an Okeanid (*Th* 357)

Phaithon (fī'-thon): son of Eos and Kephalos (not the same Phaithon who drove the chariot of the sun with disastrous results [West]) (*Th* 987)

Phasis (fa'-sis): one of the rivers that Tethys bore to Okeanos (*Th* 340)

Pherousa (fe-roo'-sə): a Nereid (*Th* 248)

Phillyra (fil'-li-rə): a nymph who bore the centaur Chiron (*Th* 1001)

Phoebe (fē'-bē): one of the Titans born to Gaia and Okeanos; the mother of Leto and Asteria (*Th* 136, 404, 409)

Phokos (fō'-kəs): ancestor of the Phokians of central Greece (West) (*Th* 1005)

Phorkys (fōr'-kis): the son of Pontos and Gaia, who, on Keto, sired a number of monsters (*Th* 238, 270, 333, 336)

Pieria (pē-âr'-ē-ə): a region immediately north of Olympos in the coastal plain of ancient Macedonia; a site that was the probable center for the worship of the Muses (*Th* 53; *WD* 1)

Pleiades (plē'-ə-dēz): a constellation of seven stars, which were originally the seven daughters of Atlas (*WD* 383, 572, 615, 619)

Ploutos (ploo'-tos): the god of wealth (*Th* 969, 971)

Pluto (ploo'-tō): an Okeanid (*Th* 356)

Polydora (pol-i-dōr'-ə): an Okeanid (*Th* 354)

Polydoros (pol-i-dōr'-os): the son of Kadmos and Harmonia (*Th* 978)

Polyhymnia (pol-i-him'-nē-ə): one of the Olympian Muses; later associated with sacred song (*Th* 78)

Pontoporea (pon-to-po-rā'-ə): a Nereid (*Th* 256)

Pontos (pon'-tos): the Sea (*Th* 107, 132, 233)

Poseidon (po-sī'-dən): brother of Zeus and god associated with the sea; called the Earth-Shaker (*Th* 15, 441, 732, 818, 930; *WD* 667)

Poulynoë (poo-lin'-ō-ē): a Nereid (*Th* 258)

Poverty: the goddess Himeros—also rendered as Hunger and Want (*Th* 592; *WD* 299, 301, 496)

Prometheus (prō-mē'-thē-əs): the son of Iapetos, who deceived Zeus (*Th* 510, 521, 536, 546, 558, 565, 614; *WD* 48, 86)

Protho (prō'-thō): a Nereid (*Th* 243)

Proto (prō'-tō): a Nereid (*Th* 248)

Protomedea (prō-to-me-dā'-ə): a Nereid (*Th* 249)

Prymno (prim'-nō): an Okeanid (*Th* 350)

Psamathe (sə-ma'-thā): a Nereid (*Th* 259, 1004)

Pytho (pī'-thō): the site of the Delphic Oracle (*Th* 499)

Rhea (rē'-ə): sister and wife of Kronos; mother of Hestia, Demeter, Hera, Hades, Poseidon, and Zeus (*Th* 135, 453, 625, 634)

Rhesus (rē'-səs): one of the rivers that Tethys bore to Okeanos (*Th* 340)

Rhodeia (ro-dā'-ə): an Okeanid (*Th* 351)

Rhodius (ro'-dē-əs): one of the rivers that Tethys bore to Okeanos (*Th* 341)

Sangarius (san-gär'-ē-əs): one of the rivers that Tethys bore to Okeanos (*Th* 344)

Sao (sou): a Nereid (*Th* 243)

Scamander (skə-man'-dûr): one of the rivers that Tethys bore to Okeanos (*Th* 345)

Selena (se-lē'-nə): goddess of the Moon (*Th* 19, 371)

Semele (se'-mə-lē): daughter of Kadmos and Harmonia, associated with the moon (*Th* 940, 976)

Simois (sim'-o-is): one of the rivers that Tethys bore to Okeanos (*Th* 342)

Sirius (sir'-ē-əs): a star in Canis Major that is the brightest in the heavens; called the dog star (*WD* 417, 587, 609)

Speio (spā'-ō): a Nereid (*Th* 245)

Sphinx: winged female monster with woman's head and lion's body (*Th* 326)

Steropes (stâr-ō'-pās): one of the three Kyklopes (Cyclops); his name means "flash" (*Th* 140)

Sthenno (sthen'-nō): one of the Gorgons (*Th* 276)

Strife: the goddess Eris (*Th* 225, 226; *WD* 11, 15, 24, 28, 803)

Strymon (stri'-mon): one of the rivers that Tethys bore to Okeanos (*Th* 339)

Styx (stix): daughter of Okeanos; a goddess associated with a river traversing the Underworld that was invoked by the gods in solemn oaths (*Th* 360, 361, 383, 389, 397, 776)

Tartaros (tär'-tə-ros): a dark, dreadful region beneath the earth; sometimes personified as a god (*Th* 119, 726, 822, 841, 852, 868)

Telegonos (te-le'-gə-nos): son of Kirke and Odysseus (*Th* 1014)

Telestho (te-les'-thō): an Okeanid (*Th* 358)

Terpsichore (tûrp-si'-khor-ē): one of the Olympian Muses, later associated with dancing and choral song (*Th* 78)

Tethys (teth'-is): daughter of Gaia and Ouranos and mother of the rivers and Okeanids (*Th* 137, 337, 346, 362, 368)

Thalia (thäl'-ē-ə): (a) one of the Olympian Muses, later associated with comedy; (b) a Nereid; (c) one of the three Graces (*Th* 77, 245, 909)

Thaumas (thou'-məs): a son of Gaia and Pontos (*Th* 238, 265, 780)

Thea (thē'-ə): daughter of Gaia and Ouranos; mother of Helios, Selena, and Eos (*Th* 135, 371, 374)

Thebes: city in Boeotia founded by Kadmos (*Th* 978; *WD* 163)

Themis (them'-is): a goddess associated with established custom and order; mother of the Hours and the Fates (*Th* 16, 135, 901)

Themisto (them-is'-tō): a Nereid (*Th* 261)

Theo (thē'-ō): an Okeanid (*Th* 354)

Thetis (thē'-tis): a Nereid; the mother of Akhilleus (*Th* 244, 1006)

Thrace: an ancient land in the Balkan peninsula (*WD* 507)

Titans: the children of Gaia and Ouranos, who ruled the earth until overthrown by the Olympian gods; the name means "strivers" or "strainers" (*Th* 208, 393, 424, 630, 632, 648, 649, 663, 668, 674, 676, 696, 717, 729, 813, 820, 851, 882)

Tritogeneia (tri-to-gə-nā'-ə): an epithet of unknown origin pertaining to Athena; it apparently means "born for three" (*Th* 895)

Triton (trī'-ton): son of Poseidon and Amphitrite (*Th* 931)

Troy: ancient city of Asia Minor (*WD* 165)

Tyche (too'-khā): an Okeanid (*Th* 360)

Typhoeus (ti-fā'-əs): a monster born from Gaia and Tartaros, who rivaled Zeus (*Th* 821, 823, 837, 869)

Typhon (tī'-fon): another name for Typhoeus (*Th* 306)

Tyrrhenians (tir-rā'-ni-ənz): another name for Etruscans (*Th* 1016)

Urania (yûr-ā'-ni-ə): (a) one of the Olympian Muses, later associated with astronomy; (b) an Okeanid (*Th* 78, 350)

Victory: the goddess Nike, a daughter of Styx (*Th* 384)

Xanthe (zan'-thē): an Okeanid (*Th* 356)

Zephyros (ze'-fi-ros): the West Wind (*Th* 379, 870; *WD* 594)

Zeus (zoos): son of Kronos (hence Kronion); the lord of the Olympian gods, who bears the aegis (emblematic shield or breastplate); sometimes referred to as the Father or the Cloud-Gatherer; referred to throughout the *Theogony* and the *Works and Days*

Zeuxo (zoox'-ō): an Okeanid (*Th* 352)